THE KINGDOM STORY
E X P E R I E N C E

SMALL GROUP STUDY

NEW TESTAMENT

DR. JOHN S. LEWIS

THE KINGDOM STORY EXPERIENCE
SMALL GROUP STUDY
THE NEW TESTAMENT

ISBN: 979-8-9871352-8-0

Book Design: Kami Wright, inMode Design + Editing, Maple Valley, WA. Illustrations: Adobe Royalty-Free

Printed in the USA by Ingram Spark, Nashville, TN.

Additional books from EQUIP and John S. Lewis

The Kingdom Story Experience — Small Group Study — The Old Testament Story

Discipleship Reframed — Building a Framework for a Culture of Disciple-Making

Three Nails, One Purpose — Following Christ to His Cross and Resurrection

Finding the Treasure in Christmas — Advent Traditions for Families with Kids of All Ages

This book is dedicated to Kingdom Story alumni

who patiently helped me discover the wings of story in my

own stony heart, and to the King of Kings, whose fingerprints

I can see from cover to cover, and who, in the words of a

famous rabbi, created you and me because...

God loves story.

MYSIA

TROAS •   • ADRAMYTTIUM

N

★ PERGAMOS

- - - - - ★ THYATIRA

★ SARDIS

SMYRA ★ ★ PHILA

★ LYDIA

★ ★ L

EPHES

COLO

MILETUS • CARIA

PATMOS •

CNIDUS

RHODES

TABLE OF CONTENTS

FOREWORD

As a pastor of a church in the first quarter of the 21st century, I have come to this regrettable conclusion: we live in a time where a significant part of Christianity in the United States is only tenuously Christian. Most self-identified Christians are disconnected from the historical tradition of faith, having exchanged the fullness of Kingdom living for (at best) an hour on Sunday. Instead of robust faith in Jesus, many settle for a pale watered-down version of the Kingdom in which Jesus invites us to participate. As a result, the Church today is in crisis.

Much of this crisis comes from a lack of Biblical foundations and transformation, which in turn has created a leadership crisis. There are many reasons why we find ourselves in this place, but among all the remedies I've experienced or explored, none hold the power of The Kingdom Story.

How do I know? Because God used *The Kingdom Story Experience* to rescue me from the kind of nominal faith that is so common today. I grew up going to church with my family, which is to say we attended weekly services and, depending on the congregation, participated in Sunday school and youth groups. As such, I knew a lot about the Bible and the classic stories that hold the imagination of an adolescent. But all those stories seemed anchored only to the past.

It wasn't until my late college years that I began to understand what it meant to have a living relationship with Christ, specifically that the Kingdom of God wasn't bound to people who lived the stories of the Bible. Rather, the Kingdom of God is a story that we are continually invited into. It is a "Kingdom" story— and it's all around us. It would be no overstatement to say that *The Kingdom Story Experience* was for me, at 23 years old, one of the most formative exercises in my faith journey.

I was serving in a parachurch youth ministry, passionate about sharing the love of Jesus, but I struggled to hold a coherent theology or integrated biblical perspective on so many issues. Where the Bible had before seemed to be just a collection of disparate stories and genres, this body of work helped me develop a holistic understanding of Scripture and then integrate my heart and head with my hands and habits. I was led to see both my ministry and my city in a new way.

When I came on staff at University Place Presbyterian Church (UPPC), I began to see the necessity of such training among our staff, younger interns, and volunteer leaders. Starting in the 1990s, from the youth department to our church at large, I have witnessed God use *The Kingdom Story Experience* with all sorts of men, women, and young people to bring life to their part in God's story.

Because the teaching connects with real world implications, participants experience the beautiful symmetry of growing in love with God while experiencing the desire to love and serve others.

I am now Senior Pastor at UPPC, and now more than ever I am convinced we need this approach toward spiritual and vocational formation. This is a resource that many churches could benefit from just as it has at UPPC.

John's leadership and writing is a treasure, and I am excited for you to know the transformation that comes with this sort of experience. *You will be forever changed because of it!*

REV. AARON STEWART
SENIOR PASTOR
UNIVERSITY PLACE PRESBYTERIAN CHURCH
UNIVERSITY PLACE, WASHINGTON

Introduction

The concept of viewing the Bible as a coherent, overarching story has gained momentum in Western Christianity, and for good reason. Stories have a unique power to captivate, helping us learn, grow, and remember. However, despite the common focus on reading and hearing scripture, there is a need for resources that deeply root believers in *discipleship* and *understanding* of God's larger, biblical story.

Since 1994, the *Kingdom Story Experience (KSE)* has aimed to fulfill this need by immersing participants in God's bigger story. Its core mission is to let the Lord's story shape lives, using the power of storytelling to create faithful disciples of Jesus. The KSE helps participants engage with the Bible not only as a text but as a *dynamic adventure*, one that influences how they live out their faith in their homes, workplaces, and communities.

This study has proven to be transformative for hundreds of participants, year after year, giving them a new (or renewed) sense of confidence and a strong faith foundation. It is more impactful when led by a facilitator and shared with at least three other participants. When these elements are in place, something very special happens. The experience becomes even more impactful, as each person's unique story contributes to a shared process of connecting with God's story. This communal aspect fosters a genuine, sometimes messy, yet deeply meaningful process. *We believe your experience with God's Kingdom Story will be unforgettable!*

Our Approach and Goals

The Bible is a rich, interconnected story, yet its complexity often makes it challenging to grasp—whether you're new to it or have been reading it for years. The KSE will guide you through key lessons carefully chosen for their historical significance and ability to illuminate the bigger picture. These stories serve like the edge pieces of a jigsaw puzzle, helping you piece together the framework of God's grand narrative and see how each part connects to reveal the fuller picture.

As you go forward, keep a few things in mind:

▶ Theologically, we aim to be Christ-centered and faithful to historic Christian orthodoxy, embracing the paradoxes and tensions of truth.

▶ Many hold misguided views of the Bible that weaken people's understanding of God and the Christian life. We believe that understanding God's full story arc can bring healing and clarity to these misperceptions.

▶ People across all cultures are captivated by stories. Our approach taps into emotions and life thoughts that simple principles and fill-in-the-blank answers cannot. We encourage and facilitate participants to step into the biblical characters' shoes and also share their own challenges or insights.

▶ The left (logical) and right (imaginative) sides of the brain are equally engaged during a story. Our imaginations are sparked, desires are stirred, and our ability to remember what we learn is enhanced. When this happens, our comprehension and conviction increase.

▶ The facilitator's role is to guide participation and vulnerability, but keep the focus on Jesus, not human ability or our behavior. Our view of faith, responsibility, and grace is enlarged when God is the hero of each story. We take God more seriously and ourselves less. This is freedom!

The Lesson Elements

Each lesson element is briefly explained below, providing participants and facilitators with a foundational overview of the purpose behind each section.

HEADER PANEL

Lessons begin with two stated purposes, a memory verse, the kingdom theme, a discipleship practice, and a prayer. While the Holy Spirit will lead participants beyond these parameters, they set the direction.

INTRODUCTION

This section provides a review of the last lesson's story and a glimpse into the next story. It also introduces the next theme and begins to connect it to our own current story.

WHAT IS YOUR EXPERIENCE?

One or two questions are offered for participants to share personal experiences related to the theme, helping prepare us to engage with the Bible passage with personal connections in mind.

THE BIGGER STORY

A specific parallel passage shows how a given story connects to other instances within the broader narrative of the Bible.

EXPLORE THE STORY

Participants will be assigned a character and explore the story through that lens. Certain characters are always considered:

▶ *Evil:* **the antagonist, the Devil,** who is always tempting, lying, and infiltrating culture and systems, constantly at odds with the advancement of God's Kingdom

▶ *Human characters:* **individuals or groups** who are actively or indirectly involved in the story

▶ *God:* **the hero protagonist** who is always God-Father, Son, or Holy Spirit

LIVE INTO THE STORY

This section offers options for discussion, personal reflection, action, and prayer. These four activities help participants connect God's character to their own stories and discover their place in His greater narrative:

▶ **God the Hero**—Exploring what we learned about God.

▶ **Our Story**—Seeking how the lessons speak to our personal experience of God's story. This question often travels full circle and explores how the lesson's truths connect with the **What Is Your Experience** question earlier in the lesson.

▶ **Reaching Others**—Finding a practical and culturally relevant implication of the lesson toward love, service, or leadership of others.

LOOKING AHEAD

The lesson closes with a bridge toward what's next in the story arc.

THEORY TO PRACTICE: *RESPONSE FOR DISCIPLES*

▶ **Prayer Ideas**—Options for a prayer experience either at the lesson's end or afterwards on their own. The goal is to encourage the practice of prayer in the life of each participant.

▶ **Action Ideas**—Practical ideas for the week ahead. The goal is to act on what was learned in a relevant way as an integral part of discipleship.

▶ **Discipleship Practice**—The lesson's defined spiritual practice explanation of *why* this practice matters today.

AT THAT TIME JESUS WAS BAPTIZED
BY JOHN IN THE JORDAN.

MARK 1:9

Disciples Walk in the Master's Steps

MARK 1:9-20

PURPOSE

1. To learn from Jesus' example what it means to be his disciple and help make disciples of others.

2. To determine a specific next step to help at least one person grow as a disciple of Jesus.

MEMORY VERSE

Jesus said to them, 'Follow me, and I will make you fish for people.' And immediately they left their nets and followed Jesus. (Mark 1:17-18)

KINGDOM THEME

Being and Making Disciples

DISCIPLESHIP PRACTICE

Mentoring

PRAYER

Jesus, you are the divine Teacher and Model. Please speak to my heart and open my mind through these four short stories in Mark. Impress me on what it means to follow and help others follow you.

Introduction

After Jesus came to earth as a baby, he spent the next few decades growing up like any other Jewish man. The Bible provides only a few glimpses into these years. His story truly takes off when, at age 30, he starts inviting people to believe and follow him (Mark 1:16-18).

While John 3:16 remains a cherished verse for many, it can often reduce being a Christian to simply acknowledging Jesus as the Son of God and going to heaven. Belief means more than just acknowledging something as true. Even Satan "believes" Jesus is God, yet he is far from being a Christian (James 2:19).

For a long time, the word Christian[1] has been used to label those who believe in Jesus. But is it the best term?[2]

In Mark 1, we find four brief stories that offer us two alternative identities. The first is found in the words the Father speaks to Jesus at his baptism: "You are my Son whom I love." In Christ, we, too, are called

---

1   The word Christian literally means "little Christ," which carries the idea of imitation, and is not far from the goal of a Jesus disciple.

2   The word *Christian* only shows up once in the New Testament (Acts 11:26) and was a name given to believers by those *outside* the church. Jesus never used this term.

children of God and beloved members of his family. The second identity is the term *disciple,* which comes from Jesus' call to the fishermen.

In Jesus' time, being a disciple meant far more than just learning information from a rabbi. It meant fully committing to imitate his lifestyle and habits. The image of an apprentice develops further what it means to be a disciple.

The twelve disciples lived with Jesus for three years, but not just to listen to his teachings. They observed and then sought to imitate how he prayed, loved, healed, taught, and so much more. Being a disciple meant learning from Jesus in a way that transformed their hearts, minds, and actions.

Jesus, as the Son of God, revealed what God is like and what it means to be fully human. While its common knowledge that he had twelve of his own disciples, the reality of Jesus as also a submitted disciple is less emphasized.

Jesus would have learned and faithfully followed the Scriptures during his first 30 years, just like any devout Hebrew male. But beyond that, he nurtured a special relationship with his heavenly Father.

At age 12, he referred to the temple as "my Father's house." As an adult, he spoke about his Father in ways that reflected the devotion of a disciple to a master: "I only do what I see the Father doing" (John 5:19).

In light of our lesson's theme, we will now read the four stories in Mark 1 from two perspectives:

1. In his baptism and wilderness experience, Jesus models for us what it means **to be a disciple** of his Father (Mark 1:9-13).

2. In his preaching and calling of the four fishermen, Jesus reveals his priority **to make disciples** (Mark 1:14-20).

These stories remind us that following Jesus is more than belief; it's about embracing our identity as children of God and living as true disciples, committed to imitating Christ and helping others do the same.

What Is Your Experience?

If being a Christian was synonymous with being a disciple of Jesus, then today's churches would swell with people growing like Jesus and actively making disciples of others. Traits or habits you would *expect* to see, but often *do not* see, in the lives of Christians include, but are not limited to:

- ▶ Obeying Jesus' teaching
- ▶ Serving specific individuals or groups
- ▶ Consistently engaging with scripture
- ▶ Growing closer to Christ through prayer

- ▶ Forgiving and reconciling with others
- ▶ Being generous with time and finances
- ▶ Experiencing Christ's healing and freedom
- ▶ Building friendships with people different from you

List several reasons why you believe churches and Christian groups struggle to make *disciples who make disciples* with traits like these.

_____

_____

_____

_____

Explore the Story

Consider the Viewpoints | Mark 1:9-20

Break up into four groups, one group for each of Mark 1:9-20's four short stories of Jesus' Beginnings (Jesus' Baptism, Testing in the Wilderness, His First Sermon, and Calling of the First Disciples). Experience the four as one continuous story. We will focus primarily on Jesus as a "disciple" of his Father and as a disciple-maker.

STORY #1: JESUS' BAPTISM

Narrator
⁹ At that time Jesus came from Nazareth in Galilee and was baptized by John in the Jordan. ¹⁰ Just as Jesus was coming up out of the water, he saw heaven being torn open and the Spirit descending on him like a dove.

Father from Heaven
¹¹ "You are my Son, whom I love; with you I am well pleased."

STORY #2: JESUS' TEMPTATION

Narrator
¹² At once the Spirit sent him out into the wilderness, ¹³ and he was in the wilderness forty days, being tempted by Satan. He was with the wild animals, and angels attended him.

STORY #3: JESUS' FIRST SERMON

Narrator
¹⁴ After John was put in prison, Jesus went into Galilee.

Jesus
¹⁵ "The time has come," he said. "The kingdom of God has come near. Repent and believe the good news!

STORY #4: JESUS CALLS FIRST DISCIPLES

Narrator
¹⁶ As Jesus walked beside the Sea of Galilee, he saw Simon and his brother Andrew casting a net into the lake, for they were fishermen.

Jesus
¹⁷ "Come, follow me," Jesus said, "and I will send you out to fish for people."

Narrator

¹⁸ At once they left their nets and followed him. ¹⁹ When he had gone a little farther, he saw James son of Zebedee and his brother John in a boat, preparing their nets. ²⁰ Without delay he called them, and they left their father Zebedee in the boat with the hired men and followed him.

MARK 1:9-20

STORY # 1: JESUS' BAPTISM (vv. 9-11)   *JESUS AS A DISCIPLE*

1. In your own words, describe what Jesus experienced from the Father as he was baptized by the Spirit. What thoughts or emotions do you think Jesus may have felt during that moment?

    _____

    _____

    _____

2. Consider Jesus as a disciple of his Father: How did this baptism experience cause him to become more prepared for what was ahead of him?

    _____

    _____

    _____

STORY #2: JESUS' TEMPTATION (vv. 12-13)   *JESUS AS A DISCIPLE*

1. Use your imagination of Jesus' wilderness experience and describe what might have been

    a. the Devil's specific lies and temptations:

    _____

    _____

    b. Jesus' thoughts, feelings or prayers:

    _____

    _____

2. Consider Jesus as a disciple of his Father: How did this wilderness experience cause him to become more prepared for what was ahead of him?

    _____

    _____

STORY #3: HIS FIRST SERMON (vv. 14-15)　　　*JESUS AS A DISCIPLE-MAKER*

1. How would you put in your own words each of the key gospel phrases below from v. 15?

    ▶ The time is fulfilled: _____

    ▶ The Kingdom of God is at hand: _____

    ▶ Repent: _____

    ▶ Believe in the gospel: _____

2. How might his message have impacted the thoughts and emotions of his Jewish listeners at the time?

    _____

    _____

    _____

    _____

STORY #4 CALLING THE FIRST DISCIPLES (vv. 16-20)　　*JESUS AS A DISCIPLE-MAKER*

1. After understanding their original meaning, rephrase each of the five key disciple-making steps Jesus modeled in a way that reflects your current context. The first one is provided as an example.

    ▶ Jesus went to where they were: *A disciple-maker has to be in proximity to build relationships and connections with potential disciples.*

    ▶ Jesus saw them: _____

    _____

    ▶ Jesus invited them to follow: _____

    _____

    ▶ The fishermen left their nets: _____

    _____

    ▶ The fishermen followed Jesus: _____

    _____

2. Which of the five steps stood out to you most (challenge, question, encouragement, etc.)? Please explain.

    _____

    _____

Paul Also Made Disciples

In 2 Timothy 2:2, Paul reveals his commitment to Jesus' way of discipleship when he admonished his disciple Timothy: "pass on what you have received (from me) to other faithful disciples who will in turn teach others." In light of this, each of us needs individuals in our lives like:

- ▸ **Paul:** a person investing in and discipling us (i.e., a coach or mentor),

- ▸ **Barnabas:** a like-minded friend walking with us to support our discipleship journey,

- ▸ **Timothy:** a person we help follow Jesus, who soon help others do the same.

Imagine what might happen if every disciple of Jesus benefited from these three kinds of people in their lives!

 # Live into the Story

Jesus

Read the four short stories of Mark 1:9-20 again with this focus: What does each story reveal to us about Jesus, as either a disciple or a disciple-maker? Write your thoughts below by completing the sentences.

▶ Jesus' baptism revealed that as a disciple he:

_____

_____

▶ Jesus' testing in the wilderness revealed that as a disciple he:

_____

_____

▶ Jesus' first sermon revealed that as a disciple maker he:

_____

_____

▶ Jesus' calling of the first disciples revealed that as a disciple maker he:

_____

_____

Our Story

To be a maturing disciple of Jesus, everyone would ideally have a Paul (someone discipling us), a Barnabas (a disciple companion), and a Timothy (someone we are discipling). Consider the first two: Who in your life can you identify as an existing or high-potential

Paul? _____

Barnabas? _____

Reaching Others

Who in your life can you identify as an existing or high-potential Timothy, someone you could help grow as both a disciple and a future disciple-maker? Please share why you chose this person.

_____

_____

_____

Close Together in Prayer

Looking Ahead

Jesus began his ministry with a hopeful proclamation: "The time has come; the kingdom of God has come near. Repent and believe the good news!" (Mark 1:15). In our next lesson, we'll journey into Luke 4, where Jesus' sermon in Nazareth opens a second window into the heart of his mission and disciple-making goals.

Theory to Practice: *Response for Disciples*

Prayer Ideas

- ▸ Thank Jesus for being your model disciple and a faithful divine master.

- ▸ Declare your trust in Jesus to change your character and lead you to make disciples of others.

- ▸ Repent of a sinful practice that is causing harm to one or more of your meaningful relationships.

Action Ideas

- ▸ Consider one intentional step toward starting or deepening a Timothy relationship, i.e., how you can help someone specific grow in their faith. Identify one short-term hope for the relationship. Be specific.

Discipleship Practice

- ▸ **Mentoring** - An experienced Jesus follower deliberately committing themselves to invest in the growth of another less mature disciple. *How?* By sharing life's failures and successes, listening and asking questions, encouragement, and challenge. *Why?* Mentoring is crucial to passing on the faith from one generation to the next, who not only grow themselves but can then go on to mentor others.

THE SPIRIT OF THE LORD HAS ANOINTED ME TO PROCLAIM GOOD NEWS TO THE POOR...AND THE YEAR OF THE LORD'S FAVOR.

LUKE 4:18-19

Jesus Declares His Purpose

LUKE 4:14-30

PURPOSE

1. To better understand Jesus' mission of bringing God's complete restoration to those who are broken and in bondage.

2. To consider how we might experience, and help others experience, God's complete restoration.

KINGDOM THEME

Restoration

PRAYER

Father, send your Spirit today to anoint me like you anointed your son Jesus. Empower me to experience the restoration of my body, mind, and soul. Inspire me to be an agent of healing and freedom in your world.

MEMORY VERSE

The Spirit of the Lord is upon me, because He has anointed me to bring good news to the poor. (Luke 4:18)

DISCIPLESHIP PRACTICE

Healing and Freedom Prayer

Introduction

After his baptism and resisting Satan's temptations in the wilderness, Jesus returned to Nazareth. As he stood on the verge of launching his kingdom ministry, Jesus delivered a powerful sermon in his hometown synagogue. In this inaugural address-type sermon, he slightly adapted Isaiah 61:1-2:

"The Spirit of the Lord is on me, because he has anointed me to proclaim good news to the poor. He has sent me to proclaim freedom for the prisoners and recovery of sight for the blind, to set the oppressed free, to proclaim the year of the Lord's favor."

Centuries earlier, these words had offered hope of restoration to the Hebrew exiles in Babylon. To those in the Nazareth synagogue, they communicated promises of healing and freedom that only the Messiah, Israel's future Savior, could fulfill.

Reading the opening verses of Isaiah 61 would have brought to the hearers' minds their wide-ranging expectations for the Messiah: physical, emotional, spiritual, mental, economic, and social restoration.

After putting down the scroll, Jesus boldly declared, *"These words have been fulfilled in your hearing."* By saying this, Jesus made it clear to the people in Nazareth that he was the long-awaited King and

Savior, the one who would fulfill Isaiah's prophecy. If Jesus' claim was true, Israel's wait for their Messiah was over. In the short term, they were bound to be disappointed.

Jews in Jesus' days expected the Messiah to arrive in splendor, wearing a crown, ready to conquer their enemies as Joshua and King David had done. He would defeat the Roman oppressors and restore Israel's national glory.

This longing for a triumphant military leader made it difficult for them to accept Jesus as the Messiah. Serious doubts about him and his mission immediately erupted.

Jesus was promising to fulfill all the Old Testament prophecies of the Messiah, including overcoming Israel's oppressors. However, this victory over evil and complete restoration will happen only on the day of his return.

Until then, we experience glimpses of restoration and place our full hope in his final coming.

Lord, ignite a movement of healing and freedom through Christ across the world, reaching hearts and restoring broken lives. Let me be a part of it.

What Is Your Experience?

What area in this present season of your life would you like to experience more of God's freedom, healing, or restoration? See below for possible examples. Circle one. Please explain your choice.

- ▶ **Physical:** illness or something not right in your body

- ▶ **Emotional:** warped feelings, oppressive memories, excessive stress or worry

- ▶ **Spiritual:** shame, sinful habits, perverted image of God

- ▶ **Social:** loneliness, needing the approval of others, fear of rejection

- ▶ **Mental:** negative images or thoughts, lies or misperceptions

- ▶ **Economic:** unemployment, pressure to perform, struggle to meet your needs

_____

_____

_____

_____

Explore the Story

Consider the Viewpoints | Luke 4:14-24

Your group leader will assign you a character from the four below. Notice what your character does and says, and then imagine their thoughts and feelings. Share some of your discussion highlights, any lingering questions, and how you can possibly relate to this character.

EVIL

The Enemy intends to use his resources to paralyze all people into some state of sickness or bondage. He equally resists God's attempts to restore those who need healing and freedom.

THE SYNAGOGUE LEADER

The synagogue leader likely watched Jesus growing up and noticed his ease with the Torah. As a Jewish religious leader, he longed for the Messiah's coming, yet he would have been fierce in protecting his flock from false teachers.

THE PEOPLE OF NAZARETH

Nazareth's everyday experiences included feeling shame for being a Jew, anger toward their Roman enemies, abandonment by God, and hunger from oppressive taxation. For nearly three decades, this community watched Jesus grow up; they had no reason to believe he was the Messiah. After his baptism and first preachings in the surrounding region, news about him quickly traveled home.

JESUS THE HERO

God's efforts to bring shalom to his children climaxed in the sending of his Spirit and anointing of his Son. Through Jesus, the Great Physician, God the Father would soon release a wave of freedom, healing, and restoration on earth.

Narrator

14 *Jesus returned to Galilee in the power of the Spirit, and news about him spread through the whole countryside.* 15 *He was teaching in their synagogues, and everyone praised him.* 16 *He went to Nazareth, where he had been brought up, and on the Sabbath day he went into the synagogue, as was his custom. He stood up to read,* 17 *and the scroll of the prophet Isaiah was handed to him. Unrolling it, he found the place where it is written and began to read:*

Jesus

18 *"The Spirit of the Lord is on me, because he has anointed me to proclaim good news to the poor. He has sent me to proclaim freedom for the prisoners and recovery of sight for the blind, to set the oppressed free,* 19 *to proclaim the year of the Lord's favor."*

(Scripture continues on the next page)

Narrator

20 Then he rolled up the scroll, gave it back to the attendant and sat down. The eyes of everyone in the synagogue were fastened on him.

Jesus

21 "Today this scripture is fulfilled in your hearing."

Narrator

22 All spoke well of him and were amazed at the gracious words that came from his lips.

People

"Isn't this Joseph's son?"

Jesus

23 "Surely you will quote this proverb to me: 'Physician, heal yourself!' And you will tell me, 'Do here in your hometown what we have heard that you did in Capernaum.' 24 Truly I tell you, no prophet is accepted in his hometown.

LUKE 4:14-24

THE BIGGER STORY

Jesus Lived Out His Purpose

In various gospel stories, Jesus fulfilled his Luke 4 promise to bring good news to the poor, freedom for the oppressed, healing to the broken, and sight to the blind. For example, in Mark 10:46-52, Jesus speaks to and heals blind Bartimaeus and invites him into a new way of thinking and experiencing relationships. Holistic ministry!

Live into the Story

> ¹⁸"The Spirit of the Lord is on me because he has anointed me to proclaim good news to the poor. He has sent me to proclaim freedom for the prisoners and recovery of sight for the blind, to set the oppressed free, ¹⁹ to proclaim the year of the Lord's favor. (Luke 4:18-19)

Jesus

1. In your own words, summarize Luke 4:18–19 and describe the kind of "good news" Jesus promised to speak and live out.

    _____

    _____

    _____

2. What do vv. 18-19 imply about the character of Jesus, our Messiah and Lord?

    _____

    _____

    _____

Our Story

1. Read Jesus' words again in Luke 4:18-19 (see above). Try to hear Jesus directly speaking to you. Remember from the **What is Your Experience** question the area of your life you wanted to experience his healing and freedom. Write it below, or note another area that has come to mind.

    _____

    _____

2. What do you imagine God's Spirit saying to you about a first step toward your journey of healing and freedom in this area? Please explain.

    _____

    _____

    _____

    _____

Reaching Others

If Jesus were walking around your community today, what are two places you would expect him to search for people who needed his healing, freedom, or restoration? Do Jesus' followers in your community spend much time in two those places? If so, please explain what they do there. If not, take a guess as to why not.

▶ Place 1: _____

_____

_____

▶ Place 2: _____

_____

_____

Close Together in Prayer

Looking Ahead

Jesus leaves Nazareth to fully step into his Spirit-empowered mission, revealing the Kingdom of God through words of truth and acts of mercy. Every teaching, healing, miracle, and deliverance flowed from his deep, unstoppable compassion. One vivid glimpse of this is the miracle of the loaves and fishes, where he met the hunger of thousands with grace and abundance.

Theory to Practice: *Response for Disciples*

Prayer Ideas

▶ Thank Jesus the Great Physician for his determination to bring us his restoration, healing, and freedom.

▶ Imagine yourself sitting in the Nazareth synagogue and Jesus pouring a large bucket of his Spirit over your head and body. You feel the flow and drops of God's presence run over unhealthy thought patterns in your mind, over old wounds in your heart, and over the fear and heaviness in your soul.

▶ Read vv. 18-19 as a prayer; ask Jesus to bring his restoration first in you and then through you to others.

Action Ideas

▶ Commit before God to pursuing Christ's freedom or healing for yourself or someone you love or serve.

▶ Write down one specific step you can take this week toward freedom or healing. Be clear about what you will do, when you will do it, and who will support or guide you in the process.

Discipleship Practice

▶ **Healing and Freedom Prayer** - When praying for individuals facing physical illness, emotional wounds, mental struggles, or spiritual oppression, we can include practices like laying on of hands, anointing with oil, imaginative prayer, and speaking words of faith and authority. *Why?* Because Jesus still desires to bring supernatural healing and freedom to his children, which is essential for us to fully become like him.

LOOKING UP TO HEAVEN, HE GAVE THANKS AND BROKE THE LOAVES.
THEN HE GAVE THEM TO HIS DISCIPLES TO DISTRIBUTE TO THE PEOPLE.

LUKE 6:41

Jesus Multiplies Loaves, Fish, and Compassion

MARK 6:30-45

PURPOSE

1. To better understand both the centrality and the ingredients of Jesus' compassion.

2. To commit to living out more of Jesus' compassion in our spheres of influence.

MEMORY VERSE

When Jesus landed and saw a large crowd, he had compassion on them, because they were like sheep without a shepherd. So he began teaching them many things. (Mark 6:34)

KINGDOM THEME

Compassion

DISCIPLESHIP PRACTICE

Solitude

PRAYER

God, I admit that the needs around me and the problems of this world can overwhelm me. Bread of Life, fill my heart with your compassion for others as I enter this story. Help me to seek to love and serve others as you did.

Introduction

In Nazareth, Jesus proclaimed his mission to bring healing freedom to those captive to sin. Through his preaching, teaching, and healing, he began to fulfill that promise, manifesting signs of God's kingdom on earth. In everything Jesus did, he demonstrated that "God so loved the world" (John 3:16).

While the cross is undoubtedly Jesus' greatest expression of love, Jesus spread God's love wherever he went.

This lesson focuses on a story that exemplifies Jesus' loving care and holistic ministry: the miraculous feeding of the multitudes. After teaching thousands about his kingdom, Jesus fed them by multiplying

a few fish and loaves of bread. This miracle reveals Christ's concern for people's various needs and calls us to do the same.[1]

The word Mark most often uses to describe Jesus' ministry is not *love* but *compassion*. This distinction is important because the word "love" can easily be misunderstood.

What precisely is compassion, and what makes it different than merely feeling sorry for someone?

---

1 This miracle story is included in all four gospels, showing the importance it played in Jesus' ministry.

In both the Old and New Testaments, compassion describes God's deep concern for his people's suffering (Exodus 34:6-7, Psalm 103:13).

Biblical compassion starts with an intense, personal identification with the suffering of others. The word "compassion" comes from two Latin roots: *com* (with) and *passion* (suffering). This is what Jesus did—he entered our world, saw our trials, felt our pain, and suffered with us.

In today's story, Jesus' compassion for the lost led him to acts of healing, teaching, and preaching.

Nowhere is this more evident than on the cross, where Jesus bore the full weight of our sin (2 Corinthians 5:21).

What does compassion look like for Jesus' disciples today?

Christ's compassion calls us first to enter into someone's pain, to deeply understand it, and finally to act.

May Christ's example lead us to worship him and then follow his path of compassion, for the lost and lonely of our world are crying out for the love only Christ can give.

What Is Your Experience?

The secret of Jesus' compassion with people was first being enveloped in his Father's love. We, too, must first receive God's compassion before it naturally flows through us. This is especially hard when we fall short or sin in some way. When you fail to love God or another person, how easily do you experience God's compassion? Please explain and give an example.

_____

_____

_____

_____

_____

_____

 # Explore the Story

Consider the Viewpoints | Mark 6:30-45

Your group leader will assign you a character from the four below. Notice what your character does and says, and then imagine their thoughts and feelings. Share some of your discussion highlights, any lingering questions, and how you can possibly relate to this character.

EVIL

The Devil's first two temptations to Jesus in the wilderness could be paraphrased like this: "Use your power for yourself—turn these stones into bread to satisfy your hunger. Or perform a public miracle—jump from the temple and let angels rescue you, so people will admire and accept you as the Messiah" (Matt. 4:3-6). It's easy to imagine the Devil echoing these same temptations throughout Jesus' ministry—and even whispering them to the Church today.

THE TWELVE DISCIPLES

After an intense short-term mission trip to the local villages, the disciples returned exhausted. Despite their lack of compassion for these new crowds, Jesus invited them to learn and participate in his miracle of "bread and fish" compassion.

THE CROWDS

These people lived in constant struggle, barely getting by under the harsh weight of Roman rule and crushing taxes. Their religious leaders piled on burdensome rules instead of offering hope or relief. But when news of Jesus' miracles and ministry spread, it sparked a glimmer of hope in their hearts: "Could this be the Messiah we've been waiting for?"

JESUS THE HERO

Jesus came to show God's love and compassion to the world. He started his ministry in Israel but soon extended his compassion to all nations through his "new body," the church.

Narrator

30 The apostles gathered around Jesus and reported to him all they had done and taught. 31 Then, because so many people were coming and going that they did not even have a chance to eat, he said to them,

Jesus

"Come with me by yourselves to a quiet place and get some rest."

(Scripture continues on the next page)

Narrator

[32] So they went away by themselves in a boat to a solitary place. [33] But many who saw them leaving recognized them and ran on foot from all the towns and got there ahead of them. [34] When Jesus landed and saw a large crowd, he had compassion on them, because they were like sheep without a shepherd. So he began teaching them many things. [35] By this time it was late in the day, so his disciples came to him and said,

Disciples

"This is a remote place, and it's already very late. [36] Send the people away so that they can go to the surrounding countryside and villages and buy themselves something to eat."

Jesus

[37] "You give them something to eat."

Disciples

"That would take more than half a year's wages! Are we to go and spend that much on bread and give it to them to eat?"

Jesus

[38] "How many loaves do you have? Go and see."

Disciples

"Five—and two fish."

Narrator

[39] Then Jesus directed them to have all the people sit down in groups on the green grass. [40] So they sat down in groups of hundreds and fifties. [41] Taking the five loaves and the two fish and looking up to heaven, he gave thanks and broke the loaves. Then he gave them to his disciples to distribute to the people. He also divided the two fish among them all. [42] They all ate and were satisfied, [43] and the disciples picked up twelve basketfuls of broken pieces of bread and fish. [44] The number of the men who had eaten was five thousand. [45] Immediately Jesus made his disciples get into the boat and go on ahead of him to Bethsaida, while he dismissed the crowd.

MARK 6:30-45

THE BIGGER STORY

Multiplying Loaves in the Early Church

In Acts 6:1–7, the early Church launched a feeding program for Greek widows—definitely less dramatic than the miracle of the loaves, but it still shares some striking similarities. Both stories overflow with compassion, involve wise delegation, address physical needs through feeding, and create space for the teaching of God's Word.

 # Live into the Story

Jesus

What might Jesus' actions throughout this miracle story tell us about his priorities and character? Please name several for each.

▶ Jesus' priorities:

_____

_____

_____

▶ Jesus' character:

_____

_____

_____

Our Story

The ingredients or steps of Jesus' compassion could be summarized in four steps:

1. **Go** to where people are suffering.

2. **See** what is happening from God's perspective.

3. **Feel** with deep empathy and identify with the one in pain.

4. **Act** in a way that helps serves the people and relieves their suffering.

Which of compassion's four steps comes to you the easiest? Which is the hardest? Please explain.

_____

_____

_____

_____

Reaching Others

Jesus desires that the miracle of compassion and acts of love continue to multiply today. Pick one of the options below and then brainstorm a specific idea for each of the four steps of compassion (**go, see, feel, do**) in the activities of

- ▶ a community food bank.

- ▶ a business committed to developing quality products and customer service.

- ▶ a family committed to loving each other and their neighbors.

Go: _____

See: _____

Feel: _____

Do: _____

Close Together in Prayer

Looking Ahead

Compassion led Jesus to teach, preach, heal and perform miracles. After three years of transforming lives, his journey brought him to Jerusalem, where a pivotal moment awaited in an upper room. Here, Jesus would offer the Twelve a profound sign of his incredible love and servant's heart, forever changing their understanding of being his disciple.

Theory to Practice: *Response for Disciples*

Prayer Ideas

▸ Ask God to help you receive his love and compassion, starting with the times and seasons you've fallen short.

▸ Confess and repent from your apathy, passivity, self-centeredness, or anything else that has blocked you from experiencing Jesus' compassion for others.

▸ Pair up with someone or gather a small group. Read Psalm 136 aloud together—one person reads the first line of each verse, and the others respond with, "His love endures forever." This powerful refrain reminds us that God's love and compassion didn't start with Jesus—it's been active since the beginning.

Action Ideas

▸ Listen to your heart and God's voice. How can you offer a specific person a "loaf" or a "fish" of compassion this week? To whom, where, and when might this best happen?

▸ Identify a time in the next week where you can set aside at least two hours to be alone with God and rest. What will that day and time be? Where will go to be fully away from people's interruptions? What will you do and *not* do to replenish your energy?

Discipleship Practice

▸ **Solitude** | Regularly removing ourselves from the presence of people to create space to experience God alone and other spiritual practices. *Why?* We want greater freedom from the lies of the enemy and from relying too much on people and their opinions. In solitude we instead cultivate a familiarity with God, his presence, and his voice.

BUT WHEN THEY CAME TO JESUS AND FOUND THAT HE WAS ALREADY
DEAD, ONE OF THE SOLDIERS PIERCED JESUS' SIDE WITH A SPEAR,
BRINGING A SUDDEN FLOW OF BLOOD AND WATER.

JOHN 19:33-34

The Passion and Purpose of the Cross

SCENES FROM MATTHEW 26-27

PURPOSE

1. To understand God's eternal and life-changing purposes in the death of his Son.

2. To know how the cross of Christ can help us better address our own sufferings and the hard questions they might raise.

KINGDOM THEME

God's Purpose in Suffering

PRAYER

Christ, Lamb of God, you who have experienced great suffering, speak to my mind. Meet me in the deepest places of my heart. In seeing your journey of the cross, prepare me to face the suffering that is either here already or sure to come.

MEMORY VERSE

When the centurion and those with him who were guarding Jesus saw the earthquake and all that had happened, they were terrified and exclaimed, 'Surely He was the Son of God!' (Matthew 27:54)

DISCIPLESHIP PRACTICE

Submission

Introduction

Unlike most biographies of famous figures, the detailed account of Jesus' death holds a dominant place in all four gospels. *So why did Matthew, Mark, Luke, and John choose to give such emphasis to it?*

Through their long accounts of Christ's death, they made it clear that the cross was and remains central to Christ's earthly purpose—his climactic accomplishment. His death demonstrated God's profound mercy through the unexpected means of suffering.

Matthew's goal in retelling the story of the cross was twofold: to strengthen the faith of the church and to address the misconceptions of skeptics. These included the ordinary Jews, the religious leaders, the zealots, and even the Roman oppressors.

The purpose of Jesus' final moments was to invite every generation to bring their sins, doubts, and suffering to the Christ of Calvary—the hill where he was crucified. It is often in that place of deepest pain and struggle that we wrestle most honestly with our questions about God.

How can a loving, all-powerful God allow suffering, or even use it as part of his divine plan?

This difficult question surfaces when we witness evil seemingly going unchecked. For many, the pain of war, disease, injustice, and death can make God seem distant, indifferent, or even cruel.

While there are no easy answers to the problem of human suffering, the gospels proclaim that God sent his Son to suffer on our behalf. His sufferings in life and death show that God fully entered into our pain—*for* us, *with* us, and even *through* us. For those who identify with Christ, these three truths offer great hope in the midst of suffering:

1. **God in Christ suffered *for* us:** God—who is all-knowing, all-powerful, and all-loving—chose to suffer on the cross through his Son for our sake. Through Christ's sacrifice, we are forgiven and restored to a relationship with the Father, Son, and Holy Spirit. *Why did he do this?* Because he loves us with an infinite love (Romans 5:8).

2. **God in Christ suffers *with* us:** Jesus, who shared in our humanity and suffering while on earth (Hebrews 2:14), now lives in us. The mystery is that Jesus continues to suffer with us as we suffer. His compassion, literally meaning "to suffer with," means that he shares in our pain.

3. **God in Christ suffers *through* us:** The apostle Paul often spoke of this profound mystery: that even after his resurrection and ascension, Jesus continues to suffer—through the sufferings of his people, his "body" on earth. Because Christ embodies compassion, and because his followers can suffer in ways that Jesus himself did not experience, Christ continues to suffer in new ways through us (Colossians 1:24).

These truths offer us a way to endure suffering with hope, knowing that Christ is not distant but intimately involved in our pain and redemption.

Four Scenes from the Crucifixion Story

The truth of God's will in Christ's death emerges from the smaller scenes of the crucifixion across all four gospels. This lesson focuses on four scenes from Matthew's account. While we won't find easy answers for life's hardships, we will be reminded of the purposes of Christ's suffering.

What Is Your Experience?

1. Think back to a difficult experience in your life story that might have caused you to doubt God's love, plan, or power. Can you now recognize at least one way that God was faithful to be with you and work something good in or through you in that time? Please explain.

_____

_____

_____

_____

_____

_____

Explore the Story

Consider the Viewpoints | Short Stories from Matthew

Break up into four groups, one group for each of these four short story scenes from Matthew (The Lord's Supper, The Gethsemane Prayer, Jesus' Anguished Cry, and the Three Signs). Experience the four as one continuous story. Then, for your assigned passage, ask: *What questions do you have after reading this passage? Who are the characters that would have been present in this scene? How might this scene encourage people who suffer today?*

SCENE 1: THE LORD'S SUPPER

Narrator

26:26 *While they were eating, Jesus took bread, and when he had given the blessing, he broke it and gave it to his disciples, saying,*

Jesus

"Take and eat; this is my body."

Narrator

27 *Then Jesus took a cup, and when he had given the blessing, he gave it to them, saying,*

Jesus

"Drink from it, all of you. 28 *This is my blood of the covenant, which is poured out for many for the forgiveness of sins.* 29 *I tell you, I will not drink from this fruit of the vine from now on until that day when I drink it new with you in my Father's kingdom."*

SCENE 2: THE GETHSEMANE PRAYER

Narrator

26:36 *Then Jesus went with his disciples to a place called Gethsemane, and he said to them,*

Jesus

"Sit here while I go over there and pray."

Narrator

37 *He took Peter and the two sons of Zebedee along with him, and he began to be sorrowful and troubled.*

Jesus

38 *"My soul is overwhelmed with sorrow to the point of death. Stay here and keep watch with me."*

(Scripture continues on the next page)

Narrator

[39] *Going a little farther, he fell with his face to the ground and prayed,*

Jesus

"My Father, if it is possible, may this cup be taken from me. Yet not as I will, but as you will."

STORY 3: JESUS' ANGUISHED CRY

Narrator

[27:45] *From noon until three in the afternoon darkness came over all the land.* [46] *About three in the afternoon[1] Jesus cried out in a loud voice,*

Jesus

"Eli, Eli, lema sabachthani? My God, my God, why have you forsaken me?"

STORY 4: THREE SIGNS

Narrator

[27:51] *At that moment the curtain of the temple was torn in two from top to bottom. The earth shook, the rocks split* [52] *and the tombs broke open. The bodies of many holy people who had died were raised to life.*

MATTHEW 26:26-29, 36-39, 27:45-46, 51-52

---

1   This was the exact time that the priests slaughtered the Passover lambs in the temple.

MATTHEW 26:26-29 | THE LORD'S SUPPER

1. Besides Jesus, who else was present in this scene? Take a moment to imagine yourself in the shoes of Jesus and those around him—how might they have experienced this moment?

    _____

    _____

    _____

2. What thoughts or feelings might they have experienced in this moment?

    _____

    _____

    _____

MATTHEW 26:36-39 | THE GETHSEMANE PRAYER

1. Take a moment to imagine yourself in the shoes of Jesus—what might he have been feeling and thinking in this time of prayer?

_____

_____

_____

2. What does this section contribute to our understanding of the purpose of Jesus' death?

_____

_____

_____

MATTHEW 27:45-46 | JESUS' ANGUISHED CRY

1. Besides Jesus, who else was present in this scene? Take a moment to imagine yourself in the shoes of Jesus and those around him—how might they have experienced this moment?

_____

_____

_____

2. What thoughts or feelings might they have experienced in this moment?

_____

_____

_____

1. Take a moment to imagine yourself among those in Jerusalem who witnessed one or more of these signs. What thoughts or emotions might have arisen as they watched them unfold?

   _____

   _____

   _____

2. What does this section contribute to our understanding of the purpose of Jesus' death?

   _____

   _____

   _____

THE BIGGER STORY

The Cross Was No Surprise to Jesus

The Gospel of Mark records Jesus sharing predictions of his death and sufferings with his disciples three times, which in Hebrew thinking means he spoke of them often (see Mark 8:31-33, 9:30-32, 10:32-34). Jesus' explicit knowledge of his impending death throughout his ministry adds another layer of insight to his preeminent life purpose.

 # Live into the Story

Jesus

Summarize how the four scenes of this lesson speak to

    a.   the purpose of Jesus' death.

_____

_____

_____

    b.   the character of Jesus revealed in these four scenes.

_____

_____

_____

Our Story

Which of the four scenes from Matthew stood out or inspired you the most? How might that scene offer guidance or truth during a time of future suffering? Please explain.

_____

_____

_____

_____

_____

Reaching Others

What is one truth from these four scenes that could help you respond to either of the reasons above? Please explain.

_____

_____

_____

_____

_____

Looking Ahead

Two days after Jesus was buried, the Father and the Spirit, in a stunning display of power and love, raised him from the dead. This moment completed Christ's work on the cross and began something that would change the trajectory of human history. Jesus conquered death and his witnessed resurrection became both a *continuation* and a *brand-new start* in his story.

Theory to Practice: *Response for Disciples*

Prayer Ideas

▶ Thank Jesus that he will be present when we endure senseless suffering.

▶ Commit to being honest with God about your doubts, like Jesus did in the Garden, when you go through trials or witness great suffering in the world.

Action Ideas

▶ Identify someone you know who needs to find hope and perspective in their suffering. Make a date to meet, be present, and listen well; if appropriate, share with them not "answers" but something that you learned in this lesson. Or you could write a note or e-mail to this person, sharing your thoughts and encouragement.

▶ Identify one action you naturally don't want to do but you know Christ or someone close to you wants you to do. Do it as an act of submission to Christ and with his help and joy.

Discipleship Practice

▶ **Submission** | Yielding one's own will, desires, and authority to God and/or others. This act reveals reverence for Christ and trust in God's sovereignty. Acts of submission extend to various aspects of life, including relationships within the church, marriage, and to earthly authorities. *Why?* Submission counters the human tendency toward control and pride, and cultivates trust in God rather than in one's own understanding.

CHRIST DIED FOR OUR SINS
AND WAS BURIED, AND HE
WAS RAISED ON THE
THIRD DAY ACCORDING
TO THE SCRIPTURES.

1 CORINTHIANS 15:3-4

The Risen Jesus Makes All Things New

JOHN 20:1-18

PURPOSE

1. To see the unexpected details of Jesus' resurrection from the perspective of those who first witnessed it.

2. To experience more of the realities of Jesus' resurrection in our lives today.

KINGDOM THEME

Resurrection

PRAYER

Father God, help me see your Son's resurrection more clearly and even hear him speak my name. Cultivate in me a greater gratitude and hunger for the many gifts this miracle makes possible.

MEMORY VERSE

For what I received I passed on to you as of first importance: that Christ died for our sins according to the Scriptures, that he was buried, that he was raised on the third day according to the Scriptures. (1 Corinthians 15:3-4)

DISCIPLESHIP PRACTICE

Worship

Introduction

On Passover Friday, the disciples' world was turned upside down. The day after Jesus' death[1] the disciples gathered together in Jerusalem. Fearful of being arrested, they mourned their crucified master, teacher, and friend behind locked doors. The one they believed would save them now lay dead in a nearby tomb.

To the disciples, their journey of following Jesus seemed to have abruptly ended with his burial.

But then came a new day—Sunday.

—————————
1   This day is called Holy Saturday in the Catholic tradition.

Our story in John 20 begins with the simple yet significant line: "Early on the first day of the week, while it was still dark…"

What might John be trying to convey about the resurrection through these carefully chosen words?

Mary left her home early in the darkness that first Easter morning. When she arrived at the empty tomb, the light of dawn—and the truth—was beginning to break through.

The phrase "the first day of the week" also links Jesus' resurrection to the first day of creation in

Genesis 1:3: "Let there be light." On both "first days," the light of God overcame the darkness (John 1:1-3).

The words "while it was still dark" declare: In this resurrection miracle, God is creating new life out of darkness and chaos.

Consider a parallel with C.S. Lewis' classic novel *The Lion, the Witch, and the Wardrobe*, where four children stumble upon a magical wardrobe that leads them into a whole new world. Similarly, in the days, weeks, and years following Jesus' death, his resurrection became a doorway that led his disciples into a world of "new creation"—a large step in God's ultimate redemption scheme.

What specific difference does his resurrection make in our lives today?

The New Testament declares the resurrection as the *cornerstone* of our faith, our hope, and all the blessings of God's new covenant with us.

John's resurrection account prepares us for the new reality where Jesus' person and power are available to all who put their trust in him.

In this present era of new creation, our Triune God is quietly working out his salvation plan in the world. But he wants our partnership in that endeavor. We are called to be Spirit-filled people, living as a visible sign of God's kingdom until the final "day" when our risen Christ returns to make all things new.

May God open our eyes, hearts, and lives to the new possibilities this second creation and the Kingdom of God now includes.

What Is Your Experience?

Think of your own experience and that of someone you know, who has not yet put their faith in Christ. What is one logical implication of believing

a) that there is no life after death and we are mere mortals, here today, gone tomorrow?

_____

_____

b) that there is life after death and a holy, loving God who awaits us?

_____

_____

Explore the Story

Consider the Viewpoints | John 20:1-18

Your group leader will assign you a character from the four below. Notice what your character does and says, and then imagine their thoughts and feelings. Share some of your discussion highlights, any lingering questions, and how you can possibly relate to this character.

EVIL

Knowing our human tendency to distrust what we have not experienced, the Devil will do whatever he can to discourage our belief in Jesus' resurrection—as well as our own.

PETER AND JOHN

Peter and John were two of those closest to Jesus. When Mary found them, they and the other disciples were likely hiding from the authorities in a Jerusalem home.

MARY MAGDALENE

Jesus freed Mary from the bondage of seven demons, and she became one of his most devoted followers. Early on that Easter Sunday, the Sabbath now over, she, along with several other women, made her way to the tomb to anoint Jesus' body (Mark 16:1).

THE RESURRECTED JESUS

How eager Jesus must have been for them to recognize him and know that he had risen, just as he promised (see Mark 8:31, 9:31, 10:33-34)! His unconventional plan designated common fishermen and a woman with an immoral history to be his resurrection's first witnesses.

Narrator
20:1 Early on the first day of the week, while it was still dark, Mary Magdalene went to the tomb and saw that the stone had been removed from the entrance. 2 So she came running to Simon Peter and the other disciple, the one Jesus loved, and said,

Mary
"They have taken the Lord out of the tomb, and we don't know where they have put him!"

Narrator
3 So Peter and the other disciple started for the tomb. 4 Both were running, but the other disciple outran Peter and reached the tomb first. 5 He bent over and looked in at the strips of linen lying there but did not go in. 6 Then Simon Peter came along behind him and went straight into the tomb. He saw the strips of linen lying there, 7 as well as the cloth that had been wrapped around Jesus' head. The cloth was still lying in its place,

(Scripture continues on the next page)

separate from the linen. [8] Finally the other disciple, who had reached the tomb first, also went inside. He saw and believed. [9] They still did not understand from Scripture that Jesus had to rise from the dead. [10] Then, the disciples went back to where they were staying.

[11] Now Mary stood outside the tomb crying. As she wept, she bent over to look into the tomb [12] and saw two angels in white, seated where Jesus' body had been, one at the head and the other at the foot.

Angels
[13] "Woman, why are you crying?"

Mary
"They have taken my Lord away and I don't know where they have put him."

Narrator
[14] At this, she turned around and saw Jesus standing there, but she did not realize that it was Jesus.

Jesus
[15] "Woman, why are you crying? Who is it you are looking for?"

Mary
"Sir, if you have carried him away, tell me where you have put him, and I will get him."

Jesus
[16] "Mary."

Mary
"Rabboni!" (Which in Aramaic means "Teacher")

Jesus
[17] "Do not hold on to me, for I have not yet ascended to the Father. Go instead to my brothers and tell them, 'I am ascending to my Father and your Father, to my God and your God.'"

Narrator
[18] Mary Magdalene went to the disciples with the news:

Mary
"I have seen the Lord!"

Narrator
And she told them that he had said these things to her.

JOHN 20:1-18

Jesus Resurrection and Our Resurrection

In 1 Corinthians 15:12ff, Paul makes a strong case: After physical death, Jesus' followers will be raised like Christ. We will even have bodies like his risen body. If Jesus was not raised from the dead, then we have no grounds for trusting God to restore our world, no hope that suffering will ever end, or that we will live after we die. Without a belief in the physical resurrection of Jesus, "we are above all people to be pitied" (1 Corinthians 15:14).

Live into the Story

Jesus

The resurrected Jesus appeared to Mary and the disciples in a body that was both familiar and transformed. From the resurrection accounts in John, we can identify several ways Jesus *remained the same* in his post-resurrection person.

- ▶ He knew their names.

- ▶ He still had a body and his hands still had the wounds from the Roman nails (John 20:25-27).

- ▶ He helped them catch fish and ate breakfast with them (John 21:4-12).

According to our John 20 story and to Luke 24:31, 36, what are several realities about Jesus that clearly *did* change?

_____

_____

_____

Reflect on one aspect of the risen Jesus described above that speaks most deeply to your everyday life of faith and hope. How might holding this truth in mind shape the way you live and trust God each day?

_____

_____

Our Story

The good news of Jesus' resurrection means

- ▶ It validates both the Old Testament prophecies and his own repeated predictions.

- ▶ It proves that he overcame death and now reigns in heaven as the King of Kings.

- ▶ It inaugurates God's new covenant with his people and his new creation in the world.

- ▶ It is the forerunner of our bodily resurrection after we die.

Which of these truths of Jesus' resurrection is currently most meaningful to you? Please explain why.

_____

_____

_____

Reaching Others

Refer back at the list of resurrection realities in the **Our Story** question above. Think of someone you care about—someone who's struggling or seeking to grow in their faith. Choose one of those resurrection realities you hope they experience. Why does that one stand out to you, and how might you share it with them?

_____

_____

_____

Close Together in Prayer

Looking Ahead

After his encounter with Mary, the resurrected Jesus appeared to his disciples behind closed doors, offering them peace and commissioning them for the mission ahead. Soon after, he met them once again, this time on the Galilean shore for a shared breakfast, where he further solidified their new mission.

Days later, Jesus ascended into heaven, leaving his disciples with a powerful promise: that they would receive the Holy Spirit. And wait they did. On Pentecost, the Spirit descended in a world-rocking display, forever empowering the disciples to carry out the mission Jesus had entrusted to them.

Theory to Practice: *Response for Disciples*

Prayer Ideas

▶ Praise God as you read Psalm 22:22–31, which is the second half of the psalm Jesus quoted on the cross. Read it as if you are the risen Jesus, now among your disciples, using this passage to help them understand what just happened. As you read, pay attention to how often worship is mentioned and what it reveals.

▶ Be thankful: What would your life be like today and after you die if you had not experienced the truth of Jesus' resurrection?

▶ Ask God's Spirit to open doors for you to experience and share the truth of Jesus' resurrection with others.

Action Ideas

▶ Read John 20:14-18. As you do, imagine yourself as Mary. Personalize the passage; hear Jesus speak your name. Then write a short prayer of worship, expressing your praise and emotions freely to the living Jesus.

▶ Write a short imaginary letter to someone who knows little about Jesus's resurrection. Include 1) some highlights or a summary of the John 20 story and 2) a truth about the resurrection you feel is important for them to know. Share the letter with someone.

Discipleship Practice

▶ **Worship** | Expressing reverence and adoration through a wide range of corporate and personal expressions: prayer, singing, scripture experiences, sacraments, silence, giving, and testimonies. *Why?* Because God's deeds and character demand to be honored. When we worship, our hearts are refreshed, realigned, and bound in common devotion with others.

SUDDENLY A SOUND
LIKE THE BLOWING
OF A VIOLENT WIND
CAME FROM HEAVEN.
THEY SAW WHAT SEEMED
TO BE TONGUES OF FIRE
CAME TO REST ON
EACH OF THEM.

ACTS 2:3-4

The Holy Spirit Comes to Dwell in Us

ACTS 2

PURPOSE

1. To understand new and promised realities the Holy Spirit made possible at Pentecost.

2. To identify a tangible impact you want the Holy Spirit to make in your life and in your faith community.

MEMORY VERSE

But you will receive power when the Holy Spirit has come upon you, and you will be my witnesses in Jerusalem, in all Judea and Samaria, and to the ends of the earth. (Acts 1:8)

KINGDOM THEME

Holy Spirit

DISCIPLESHIP PRACTICE

Faith Community

PRAYER

Father God, thank you for the truth that anyone can receive the Holy Spirit in their heart through faith in your Son, Jesus Christ. Spirit, fill me now afresh. Impart the wisdom and power I need to experience your abundant life.

Introduction

What labor pains are to the dramatic moment of a child's birth, so the 1500 years of Israel's painful history were to the climactic coming of Jesus to earth. Beyond the drama of his life, death, and resurrection, more of God's birthing was yet to come: *Pentecost.*

Let's set the stage.

Jesus gathered his disciples during the Last Supper and shared some of his most important teachings. He left them a plan to continue to" follow" him and go out to all nations as his ambassadors. Jesus assured them his leaving would be for their good; only then could he pour out the Holy Spirit to

dwell in their hearts and create his new covenant community. Through the Spirit as Helper, Jesus would continue to work in their midst (John 14:16, 23; 16:28). Their baptism in the Spirit made available the intimate fellowship Jesus shared with the Father (John 14:16, 18, 15:4-5, 17:21, 23).

Jesus shared these promises and plans with the Twelve, endured the cross, and rose from the dead.

Before he ascended to heaven, he asked the disciples to remain in Jerusalem and wait for the promised presence and power of the Holy Spirit. Joined in an upper room by over 100 other believers, they waited and prayed there for many days.

On the day of Pentecost, Jesus poured out the Holy Spirit that he received from the Father (Acts 2:32-33). His Spirit came like flames of fire, resting first on all those waiting and praying and later in the hearts of all who believed Peter's message. The Holy Spirit bestowed gifts, insights, and power—all signs of Christ's new way of being present in their lives.

The disciples began speaking in the native languages of thirteen nearby regions. All bore witness of the "mighty works of God!" (Acts 2:7-12). The indwelling Spirit also empowered the early church believers to obey God's commands and to grow in the fruit of the Spirit (Galatians 5:22-25).

Was God's Spirit only for the disciples, only for the Jews who believed in Jesus?

No, not at all. God's kingdom plan for the world's salvation (Ephesians 1:3-6) started with the nation of Israel, deepened at the coming of Jesus, and climaxed at Pentecost in the Spirit filling people from every nation.

Every group of Spirit-filled followers would be called the church, the body of Christ.

In the first thirteen chapters of Acts, the Holy Spirit is active in a fresh way and referenced more forty times; the Book of Acts could be described as the acts of the Holy Spirit that opened up Jesus' good news to the world and kingdom.

Does the Holy Spirit who came still come today and transform the lives of Jesus followers?

Yes! The Spirit who inaugurated the New Covenant can still transform hearts of stone and rebellion to hearts of flesh and ready obedience. Day by day, we, too, can live and walk by the Spirit of Jesus (Exodus 36:25-27, Galatians 5:24-25, Romans 12:1-2).

One person whose life was transformed by God's indwelling Spirit was Peter. In mere weeks, he went from a denier of Jesus to being the church's confident leader.

Good news: Like Peter and the early disciples, we cannot make a lasting influence solely by human effort. The Holy Spirit makes our love for one another visible, our witness compelling, and our disciple-making journey transforming (John 13:34-35, Matthew 28:19, Acts 1:8).

May our experience of Pentecost awaken us afresh to the difference the indwelling Holy Spirit can make in our lives—our minds, wills, emotions, and even our physical bodies.

What Is Your Experience?

When God fills new followers with his Spirit, what tangible difference(s) could it make over time in their hearts and actions? List several for each below and then consider where and how often you see these "signs" in Jesus followers.

▶ Differences in our *heart:*

_____

_____

▶ Differences in our *actions:*

_____

_____

Explore the Story

Consider the Viewpoints | Acts 2:1-47

Your group leader will assign you a character from the four below. Notice what your character does and says, and then imagine their thoughts and feelings. Share some of your discussion highlights, any lingering questions, and how you can possibly relate to this character.

EVIL

As soon as Jesus rose victorious over death, the Devil worked overtime to try and keep the New Covenant church movement from taking away his territory. Doubt and passivity were (and still are) two of his weapons.

THE JEWS WHO SAW SIGNS AND HEARD PETER'S SERMON

Most of the international Passover crowd had seen or heard of Jesus—his dramatic entry into Jerusalem, his bold teaching in the temple, his confrontation with the money changers, and ultimately, his death on the cross. Some may have even caught whispers of his rumored resurrection. So when the miracle of Pentecost burst onto the scene, word spread quickly and drew a crowd eager to understand what was happening.

PETER

After hearing Jesus' final words and watching him ascend to heaven, Peter, along with the other disciples, waited together as commanded. They were holding on to the promise that Jesus would soon fill them with his Spirit.

THE HOLY SPIRIT

The Spirit of God hovered at Creation like a mother hen over the "nest" of the chaotic waters, preparing to create a new world (Genesis 1:2). In a similar way at Pentecost, the Holy Spirit "hovered" over the room of confused disciples through whom he would create his church. With people of many languages hearing one gospel message, the Holy Spirit was preparing the church to fulfill the promises given to Abraham: "I will bless you to be a blessing to the nations."

Narrator

2:1 *When the day of Pentecost came, they were all together in one place.* 2 *Suddenly a sound like the blowing of a violent wind came from heaven and filled the whole house where they were sitting.* 3 *They saw what seemed to be tongues of fire that separated and came to rest on each of them.* 4 *All of them were filled with the Holy Spirit and began to speak in other tongues as the Spirit enabled them.* 5 *Now there were staying in Jerusalem God-fearing Jews from every nation under heaven.* 6 *When they heard this sound, a crowd came together in bewilderment, because each one heard their own language being spoken.* 7 *Utterly amazed, they asked:*

Jews from All Nations

"Aren't all these who are speaking Galileans? ⁸ Then how is it that each of us hears them in our native language? ⁹ Jews and converts to Judaism from Parthians, Medes and Elamites; residents of Mesopotamia, Judea and Cappadocia, Pontus and Asia, ¹⁰ Phrygia and Pamphylia, Egypt and the parts of Libya near Cyrene; visitors from Rome; ¹¹ Cretans and Arabs—we hear them declaring the wonders of God in our own tongues! What does this mean?"

Other Jews

¹³ "They have had too much wine."

Peter

¹⁴ "Fellow Jews and all of you who live in Jerusalem, let me explain this to you; listen carefully to what I say. ¹⁵ These people are not drunk, as you suppose. It's only nine in the morning! ¹⁶ No, this is what was spoken by the prophet Joel: ¹⁷ In the last days, God says, I will pour out my Spirit on all people... ²¹ And everyone who calls on the name of the Lord will be saved. ²² Fellow Israelites, listen to this: Jesus of Nazareth was a man accredited by God to you by miracles, wonders and signs, which God did among you through him, as you yourselves know. ²³ This man was handed over to you by God's deliberate plan and foreknowledge; and you, with the help of wicked men, put him to death by nailing him to the cross. ²⁴ But God raised him from the dead, freeing him from the agony of death, because it was impossible for death to keep its hold on him... ³² God has raised this Jesus to life, and we are all witnesses of it. ³³ Exalted to the right hand of God, he has received from the Father the promised Holy Spirit and has poured out what you now see and hear... ³⁶ "Therefore let all Israel be assured of this: God has made this Jesus, whom you crucified, both Lord and Messiah."

Narrator

³⁷ When the people heard this, they were cut to the heart and said to Peter and the other apostles,

The Jews

"Brothers, what shall we do?"

Peter

³⁸ "Repent and be baptized, every one of you, in the name of Jesus Christ for the forgiveness of your sins. And you will receive the gift of the Holy Spirit. ³⁹ The promise is for you and your children and for all who are far off—for all whom the Lord our God will call. ⁴⁰ Save yourselves from this corrupt generation."

Narrator

⁴¹ Those who accepted his message were baptized, and about three thousand were added to their number that day. ⁴² They devoted themselves to the apostles' teaching and to fellowship, to the breaking of bread and to prayer. ⁴³ Everyone was filled with awe at the many wonders and signs performed by the apostles. ⁴⁴ All the believers were together and had everything in common. ⁴⁵ They sold property and possessions to give to anyone who had need. ⁴⁶ Every day they continued to meet together in the temple courts. They broke bread in their homes and ate together with glad and sincere hearts, ⁴⁷ praising God and enjoying the favor of all the people. And the Lord added to their number daily those who were being saved.

ACTS 2:1-47

Genesis 11 and Acts 2 Compared

The Acts 2 Pentecost and Genesis 11 Tower of Babel stories share various similarities and reversals, which point to something important about the meaning of Pentecost.

The Tower of Babel story (read Genesis 11) follows the more familiar story of Noah and the flood (Genesis 6-8) and reveals the worldwide low point of sin's consequences. The Jews present on Pentecost would have been very familiar with this Tower story, and the early church would not miss its similarities with the events of Pentecost.

The Holy Spirit's coming revealed the next dramatic chapter of reversing sin's consequences from the Garden of Eden and the Tower of Babel. This can be seen more clearly by comparing the similarities and contrasts between the two stories in the table below.

Tower of Babel Genesis 11	Pentecost Acts 2
People come from all over to gather in one common place, and they speak one common language.	Similarly, Jews gather in Jerusalem from many nations; though they speak many different native languages, they as Jews speak one language: Hebrew/Aramaic.
The people who gather are confident they can reach heaven and God with their own power, gifts, efforts, and abilities.	In contrast, Jesus' followers gathered in a room are praying, desperate for God to act. They are acutely aware that they cannot acquire the gift of God's Spirit on their own.
The people ended up being scattered over the earth and now speak different languages, so they could not understand each other.	In contrast, the people from many nations each hear the same message in the tongue of their own particular language. They are united in their response of believing the gospel. They scatter to their own countries when Pentecost is over.
In the end, chaos and babbling rules over the world's scattered people.	In contrast, what first appeared to be chaos during Jesus' final days and the arrival of the Spirit actually led to the formation of a loving and unified new community—the church of Jesus Christ.

When the 120 were all in one place speaking one message in different languages, people asked "what does this mean" (Acts 1:12). We are to see that the answer partly lies in the world impact of the Tower of Babel's reversal.

Live into the Story

God the Spirit

▶ He came like wind and fire to dwell within the gathered disciples (vv. 1-2).

▶ He enabled them to speak in tongues and declare God's works in the languages of those present (vv. 3-11).

▶ He empowered Peter to preach with clarity and power.

▶ He came as promised by the prophet Joel to be poured out on all people (vv. 17-21).

▶ He moved the hearts of the skeptical crowd to hear, believe, and repent (v. 37).

▶ He will bring salvation for all who believe in Jesus (vv. 38-39).

▶ He empowered them to live radically together in community, sharing meals, prayers, and possessions (vv. 42-47).

▶ He created the community called the body of Christ, the new Israel, what we call the church.

▶ He performed miracles through the apostles that created awe among the people.

What do all these actions reveal to us about the character of the Holy Spirit? Write at least three descriptions.

*The Holy Spirit is...*_____

_____

_____

_____

Our Story

Look back at your responses to the **What Is Your Experience?** question. Choose one area from your response that you would like to grow or experience more. Why did you choose this, and what might growth look like for you?

_____

_____

_____

_____

_____

Reaching Others

1. Acts 2 describes a powerful mix of divine miracles and human actions—God's Spirit at work alongside preaching, prayer, communion, and generosity. Today, churches and Christian communities often lean too heavily toward relying only on the Holy Spirit or over-emphasizing human effort. Which tendency best describes your church or ministry context? Please explain.

   _____

   _____

2. Why might this imbalance matter, especially in the long run?

   _____

   _____

   _____

Close Together in Prayer

Looking Ahead

The outpouring of the Spirit at Pentecost and its many blessings, was never meant to be limited to the church in Jerusalem. God's intent was always global—his presence and power shared with every nation (Acts 1:8). Yet in the early days, the church remained hesitant to move beyond familiar ground. What held them back? And how did the gospel begin to break through borders and barriers to reach the world? That story is about to unfold.

Theory to Practice: *Response for Disciples*

Prayer Ideas

▸ Read Psalm 51:10 and join the Psalmist in asking for this work of the Spirit in you.

▸ Praise Father God, Lord Jesus, and the Holy Spirit for giving you dramatic moments and doing his slower work of transformation.

▸ Lift an area of your life to God where you need the Spirit's transforming power.

Action Ideas

▸ Make a list of two or more friends that you would be willing to invite to an extended prayer meeting. Let Acts 2 lead you in how to put a little structure to the time. Then follow through and organize the gathering.

▸ Read through Acts 2:42-47 and pick out one community activity of the early church that you have experienced already and then one you would now like to experience more. What's the first step you can take in that new community-building activity? Write it out and be specific.

Discipleship Practice

▸ **Faith Community** | Disciples choose to meet regularly to share life, grow in faith, and pursue God's mission together. These gatherings are marked by mutual support, vulnerability, accountability, and much more. *Why?* Because consistent relationships help us resist isolation, grow to be more like Jesus, and show his love to a world that's paying attention.

MYSIA

TROAS

ADRAMYTTIUM

PERGAMOS

★ THYATIRA

★ SARDIS

★ PHILAD

SMYRA

LYDIA

H

★ LA

EPHES

★

COLOS

CARIA

MILETUS

PATMOS

CNIDUS

RHODES

"ONE DAY AT ABOUT THREE IN THE AFTERNOON CORNELIUS HAD A VISION. HE DISTINCTLY SAW AN ANGEL OF GOD..."

ACTS 10:3-4

Christ's Invitation Is Open to All

ACTS 10

PURPOSE

1. To understand God's commitment to breaking down every barrier that would exclude anyone from his welcome and his church.

2. To take the next step in seeing our prejudices and walking the journey of reconciliation with others.

KINGDOM THEME

Reconciliation

MEMORY VERSE

Then Peter began to speak to the Gentiles gathered, "I now truly understand that God shows no partiality." (Acts 10:34)

DISCIPLESHIP PRACTICE

Reconciliation

PRAYER

God, please use this story to help me better see the barriers that keep me from embracing others I would rather avoid. Make me like Peter: open to hearing, repenting, and reconciling with others. Enlarge, Lord, the circle of whom I love.

Introduction

At Pentecost, God endowed the disciples with the promised Holy Spirit, enabling them to fulfill his command to be witnesses to the world (Acts 1:8). After this profound "vertical" experience with God, the gospel spread rapidly throughout Jerusalem and the neighboring towns.

The early church began to take shape with new converts joining daily, repenting of their sins, and placing their hope in God.

For the first time, God's people experienced the realities of the Holy Spirit and the New Covenant. The Spirit began to free them from Pharisaic legalism and the bondage of sinful desires. Their union with Christ could give them direct fellowship with God the Father. However, God's long-term plan to share his salvation blessings with all people—through radical, boundary-breaking love—faced a pervasive and formidable obstacle.

Though Pentecost brought the Jewish believers together in unity, prejudice still ran deep in the Jerusalem church. Even Peter, their leader, was not exempt. Like most Jewish men, he grew up hearing prayers like, "Lord God, thank you that you did not make me a Gentile, a slave, or a woman."

For social, religious, and racial reasons, Gentiles from other nations were not seen as equals. In Peter's mind, this judgment extended to the church. It's tough to admit, but these early disciples held prejudices.

The Jewish believers needed a "horizontal" conversion—learning to love all their neighbors.

In Israel's early history, God had required separation from idol-worshiping neighbors for the sake of holiness, identity, and survival. Gentiles could worship God as "God-fearers" and even enter the temple, but only as far as the outer court. Over time, this separation reinforced Israel's disdain toward the Gentiles.

However, the new church could not grow or reflect God's full heart if Jewish Christians refused to break down this barrier. Like today, they struggled to shed their old ways of intolerance and prejudice.

What did God do? He took dramatic action—starting directly at the head of the church with Peter.

Acts 10 tells of God visiting Cornelius, a Gentile God-fearer and Roman centurion, in a vision. Cornelius represented the power that oppressed the Jew, but still his prayers pleased God (Acts 10:2, 4). Nevertheless, he and others like him were not considered full equals to Jewish believers.

God then visited Peter in a vision. The same Jesus who ate with sinners, touched lepers, and honored women now commanded Peter to set aside his refusal to associate with Gentiles. He called him to lead the church in loving all people.

None of us are immune to prejudice, whether in Peter's time or our own. Across the world, people remain suspicious, arrogant, unloving, or even violent toward those different from themselves. Divisions emerge: men versus women, young versus old, Muslim versus Christian, black versus white, immigrant versus native, straight versus gay, urban versus rural. The list goes on.

God's command calls his people to move beyond our sinful, embedded divisions. His Spirit empowers us to model radical love and demonstrate Jesus' path of reconciliation.

Imagine the slice of heaven that would touch our world if we all experienced the same transformation Peter did.

What Is Your Experience?

Name a group of people that you or your peers tend to judge or avoid. Then name several reasons (fear, anger, discomfort, misperceptions, etc.) for judging or avoiding this "other" group of people.

▶ Group of people: _____

▶ Reasons for judging:

_____

_____

_____

Explore the Story

Consider the Viewpoints | Acts 10:1-48

Your group leader will assign you a character from the four below. Notice what your character does and says, and then imagine their thoughts and feelings. Share some of your discussion highlights, any lingering questions, and how you can possibly relate to this character.

EVIL

Since the Fall, sin has led us to experience broken relationships with God and people. The Enemy does all he can to divide people from God and each other. Sin leads groups, institutions, and individuals to naturally build walls rather than bridges.

CORNELIUS

As a member of the Roman army, Cornelius was well-trained to respect and fear a commanding officer. This posture likely affected the way he related to God. Knowing he was repugnant to the Jews, he was nevertheless determined to ask Peter for help and answers.

PETER

Though Jesus modeled radical reconciliation for him, Peter continued to rely on his religious understanding of the Gentiles. His prejudice and perspective needed to turn 180 degrees if the church was to move forward in its worldwide mission.

GOD THE HERO

God orchestrated dramatic signs to draw Peter into his mission to the Gentiles. He gave parallel visions to Peter and Cornelius, then confirmed them through the unexpected arrival of Cornelius's servants. Before repentance, prayer, or baptism, the Holy Spirit fell on the Gentiles. In this way, God welcomed them fully into his family.

Narrator

10:1 At Caesarea there was a man named Cornelius, a centurion in what was known as the Italian Regiment.

2 He and all his family were devout and God-fearing; he gave generously to those in need and prayed to God regularly. 3 One day at about three in the afternoon he had a vision. He distinctly saw an angel of God, who came to him and said,

Angel

"Cornelius!"

(Scripture continues on the next page)

Narrator

Cornelius stared at him in fear and then asked,

Cornelius

4 "What is it, Lord?"

Angel

"Your prayers and gifts to the poor have come up as a memorial offering before God. 5 Now send men to Joppa to bring back a man named Simon who is called Peter. 6 He is staying with Simon the tanner, whose house is by the sea."

Narrator

7 When the angel who spoke to him had gone, Cornelius called two of his servants and a devout soldier who was one of his attendants. 8 He told them everything that had happened and sent them to Joppa. 9 About noon the following day as they were on their journey and approaching the city, Peter went up on the roof to pray. 10 He became hungry and wanted something to eat, and while the meal was being prepared, he fell into a trance. 11 He saw heaven opened and something like a large sheet being let down to earth by its four corners. 12 It contained all kinds of four-footed animals, as well as reptiles and birds.

A Voice from Heaven

13 "Get up, Peter. Kill and eat."

Peter

14 "Surely not, Lord! I have never eaten anything impure or unclean."

A Voice from Heaven

15 "Do not call anything impure that God has made clean."

Narrator

16 This happened three times, and immediately the sheet was taken back to heaven. 17 While Peter was wondering about the meaning of the vision, the men sent by Cornelius found out where Simon's house was and stopped at the gate. 18 They called out, asking if Simon who was known as Peter was staying there. 19 While Peter was still thinking about the vision, the Spirit said to him,

The Holy Spirit

"Simon, three men are looking for you. ²⁰ So get up and go downstairs. Do not hesitate to go with them, for I have sent them."

Peter To the Men

²¹ *"I'm the one you're looking for. Why have you come?"*

The Men

²² *"We have come from Cornelius the centurion. He is a righteous and God-fearing man, who is respected by all the Jewish people. A holy angel told him to ask you to come to his house so that he could hear what you have to say."*

Narrator

²³ *Then Peter invited the men into the house to be his guests. The next day Peter started out with them, and some of the believers from Joppa went along. ²⁴ The following day he arrived in Caesarea. Cornelius was expecting them and had called together his relatives and close friends. ²⁵ As Peter entered the house, Cornelius met him and fell at his feet in reverence. ²⁶ But Peter made him get up.*

Peter

"Stand up," he said, "I am only a man myself."

Narrator

²⁷ *While talking with him, Peter went inside and found a large gathering of people.*

Peter

²⁸ *"You are well aware that it is against our law for a Jew to associate with or visit a Gentile. But God has shown me that I should not call anyone impure or unclean. ²⁹ So when I was sent for, I came without raising any objection. May I ask why you sent for me?"*

Cornelius

³⁰ *"Three days ago I was in my house praying at this hour, at three in the afternoon. Suddenly a man in shining clothes stood before me ³¹ and said, 'Cornelius, God has heard your prayer and remembered your gifts to the poor. ³² Send to Joppa for Simon who is called Peter. He is a guest in the home of Simon the tanner, who lives by the sea.' ³³ So I sent for you immediately, and it was good of you to come. Now we are all here in the presence of God to listen to everything the Lord has commanded you to tell us."*

Peter

34 "I now realize how true it is that God does not show favoritism, 35 but accepts from **every** nation the one who fears him and does what is right. 36 You know the message God sent to the people of Israel, announcing the good news of peace through Jesus Christ, who is Lord of **all**. 37 You know what has happened throughout the province of Judea, beginning in Galilee after the baptism that John preached— 38 how God anointed Jesus of Nazareth with the Holy Spirit and power, and how he went around doing good and healing **all** who were under the power of the devil, because God was with him. 39 We are witnesses of everything he did in the country of the Jews and in Jerusalem. They killed him by hanging him on a cross, 40 but God raised him from the dead on the third day and caused him to be seen. 41 He was not seen by **all** the people, but by witnesses whom God had already chosen—by us who ate and drank with him after he rose from the dead.

42 He commanded us to preach to the people and to testify that he is the one whom God appointed as judge of the living and the dead. 43 **All** the prophets testify about him that **everyone** who believes in him receives forgiveness of sins through his name."

Narrator

44 While Peter was still speaking these words, the Holy Spirit came on all who heard the message. 45 The circumcised believers who had come with Peter were astonished that the gift of the Holy Spirit had been poured out even on Gentiles. 46 For they heard them speaking in tongues and praising God.

Peter

47 "Surely no one can stand in the way of their being baptized with water. They have received the Holy Spirit just as we have."

Narrator

48 So he ordered that they be baptized in the name of Jesus Christ. Then they asked Peter to stay with them for a few days.

ACTS 10:1-48

Peter and Old Testament Jonah

The Jews' aversion to the Gentiles started centuries before the book of Acts. The Old Testament story of Jonah rebuked Israel for their hatred of the gentile Assyrians. When Jonah heard God's call to preach to the city of Nineveh, he went to Joppa instead to catch a boat going the opposite direction of Assyria; Jonah didn't want his Gentile enemies to repent and become part of God's people! It was no accident that, in Acts 10, Peter was dwelling in Joppa, that same city. No surprise either that God's Spirit led Peter to respond differently than Jonah!

Live into the Story

God

Reflect on all that our reconciling God did in this story. What do God's words and actions in our story suggest about God's character and the ministry of the Holy Spirit? List several for each below.

▶ God's character:

_____

_____

_____

_____

▶ Ministry of the Holy Spirit:

_____

_____

_____

_____

Our Story

Peter's transformation of his prejudice took place in just a few days—a miracle that often takes Jesus' followers years, if it happens at all. How open are you to beginning or deepening your commitment to let God tear down any "walls" of prejudice in your own heart? If you're willing, what is one misperception or bias about another group that you may need God's help to release? Please be as specific as you can.

_____

_____

_____

_____

Reaching Others

To help ourselves and others in this reconciliation process, we must see and then address the source of our own prejudices. Consider:

- ▶ Voices from our neighborhood, school, or church, especially from leaders and those who are just like us

- ▶ Cultural traditions

- ▶ How our parents spoke, acted, and raised us

- ▶ How our role models spoke and acted

- ▶ Social media, movies, shows, news sources

- ▶ Our own negative and "natural" feelings we have toward another group

Pick two of the bulleted sources above. Identify a specific message you have received from them.

Source #1: _____

Message: _____

Source #2: _____

Message: _____

Close Together in Prayer

Looking Ahead

In Acts 9–15, the Spirit the gates threw wide open for the gospel to spread beyond the Jews and Jerusalem. What began as a small Jewish movement gained unstoppable momentum across the Roman Empire. Led by Paul and his team, the early church stepped boldly into this mission, bringing the good news of Christ to Gentile cities—even to Athens, a city echoing with the voices of ancient thinkers searching for lasting truth.

Theory to Practice: *Response for Disciples*

Prayer Ideas

▸ Thank God for his reconciling heart made most visible in the work of the Holy Spirit.

▸ Confess any active prejudice that God has revealed within you.

▸ Ask our God, who has no walls, to bring to your mind someone from your neighborhood, workplace, school, etc., who is of a different race, orientation, or religion, someone you can choose to welcome.

Action Ideas

▸ Identify a first step you could take this week toward building a relational bridge with someone of a different background, culture, or religion. Be as specific as you can. Take that first step.

Discipleship Practice

▸ **Reconciliation** | Reconciliation restores broken relationships and heals divisions between individuals and God. It seeks to address the harm done, make amends, and rebuild trust. *Why?* Reconciliation fulfills the gospel's demand for justice and unity, breaks cycles of hurt and conflict, fosters radical love amongst believers, and offers a witness to our broken world.

MYSIA
ADRAMYTTIUM
PERGAMOS
THYATIRA
SARDIS
SMYRA
LYDIA
CARIA
MILETUS
PATMOS
CNIOUS
RHODES

WHAT YOU NOW WORSHIP AS THE UNKNOWN GOD, I AM GOING TO PROCLAIM TO YOU.

ACTS 17:23

Paul Makes Jesus Known in Athens

ACTS 17:16-34

PURPOSE

1. To better understand Paul's ministry model that launched the early church's rapid expansion into the cities of the Gentile world.

2. To see the relevance of this model for reaching distinct groups of people who are ignorant or indifferent to Jesus' message.

MEMORY VERSE

What you now worship as the unknown God, I am going to proclaim to you. (Acts 17:23)

KINGDOM THEME

Jesus' Model for Reaching Others

DISCIPLESHIP PRACTICE

Making the Gospel Relevant

PRAYER

Thank you Jesus, incarnate God, for reaching out in ways and words people can understand. Lord, equip me to be more like you so I can be involved in your life-changing ministry to others.

Introduction

The miracle of the Spirit's coming brought Jesus' good news, gifts, and transformation closer to the whole world. The Holy Spirit freed Peter from his prejudice against the Gentiles (Acts 10).

When Peter ministered to Cornelius and his Gentile friends, it sent ripples of rumors and change throughout the Jerusalem church. A council was convened, eventually deciding that full obedience to Jewish law would no longer be required for new converts. Peter remained in Jerusalem, focusing on the Jewish believers there.

Meanwhile, a former devout Jew and persecutor of Christians, Saul, had his own divine encounter and became Paul—Christ's apostle to the Gentiles (Acts 9). The world would never be the same again.

In the years that followed, God's Spirit used Paul and his team to propel the comfortable Jerusalem church into the cities of the Roman Empire.

How did Paul and his team engage these new places and quickly launch the new church into a worldwide movement?

God's evangelistic strategy led Paul to focus on key urban centers. In these bustling cities, Jews and Gentiles from many nations mingled, busying themselves with commerce, religion, politics, and pleasure. These cities, with their institutions and social networks, became strategic launching points for the church's growth. The church's influence spread swiftly through the interconnected urban hubs.

Does this emphasis on reaching cities still hold true today?

Millions of people from diverse backgrounds continue to migrate into the world's crowded cities. Culture is born and reshaped in the institutions of these urban centers, where the powerful and powerless alike gather, and humanity's greatest needs and resources converge.

Cities remain crucial for the church and the expansion of God's kingdom.

The Acts 17 story also highlights that God was preparing the city long before Paul and his team arrived in Athens. The Holy Spirit was already at work amidst the people's misguided search for God through their idols, altars, and superstitions.

God is in charge of reaching the world and invites us to partner with him.

Paul followed in the footsteps of Jesus. He entered the city as a witness, walking among the people, observing, and listening closely. In his speech, he used references they understood and built on the truths they already knew.

Paul and the early church's approach to effective multiplication prompts an important question:

How can we, filled and transformed by God's Spirit, reach the people with whom we live, work, and serve in a similar, compelling way?

Paul's words and example in Athens models the path forward.

What Is Your Experience?

Name a people group in your community that has reason to be resistant to knowing the reality of Jesus Christ. Identify several historical experiences, cultural realities, or personal beliefs that might make this group particularly resistant.

_____

_____

_____

_____

_____

_____

_____

Explore the Story

Consider the Viewpoints | Acts 17:16-34

Your group leader will assign you a character from the four below. Notice what your character does and says, and then imagine their thoughts and feelings. Share some of your discussion highlights, any lingering questions, and how you can possibly relate to this character.

EVIL

One of the Enemy's tools is to use reason to erect intellectual barriers that can create resistance toward Jesus and his gospel.

ATHENIAN PHILOSOPHERS

Large cities invite diversity on many social levels: upbringing, ideology, sexual preference, religion, language, race—you name it. Athens was no exception. Four groups of people in our story—Stoics, Epicureans, Agnostics, and Jews—represent some of the city's variety.

PAUL

Paul grew up as a Jew, living in a Greek city and studying Jewish religion, Greek philosophy, and customs. These experiences prepared him well for his bicultural ministry to Jews and Greeks and for reaching out to cities like Athens.

GOD THE HERO

Whatever satisfaction people seek from the idols and false gods of this world can only be found in Jesus. From the beginning, God has wanted all people to turn their loyalty towards him, and there alone find life.

Narrator

16 While Paul was waiting for them in Athens, he was greatly distressed to see that the city was full of idols.

17 So he reasoned in the synagogue with both Jews and God-fearing Greeks, as well as in the marketplace day by day with those who happened to be there. 18 A group of Epicurean and Stoic philosophers began to debate with him. Some of them asked,

Athenian Philosophers

"What is this babbler trying to say? He seems to be advocating foreign gods."

Narrator

They said this because Paul was preaching the good news about Jesus and the resurrection. 19 Then they took him and brought him to a meeting of the Areopagus, where they said to him,

Athenian Philosophers

"May we know what this new teaching is that you are presenting? 20 You are bringing some strange ideas to our ears, and we would like to know what they mean." 21 (All the Athenians and the foreigners who lived there spent their time doing nothing but talking about and listening to the latest ideas.)

Paul

22 "People of Athens! I see that in every way you are very religious. 23 For as I walked around and looked carefully at your objects of worship, I even found an altar with this inscription: to an unknown god. So you are ignorant of the very thing you worship—and this is what I am going to proclaim to you.

24 The God who made the world and everything in it is the Lord of heaven and earth and does not live in temples built by human hands. 25 And he is not served by human hands, as if he needed anything. Rather, he himself gives everyone life and breath and everything else. 26 From one man he made all the nations, that they should inhabit the whole earth; and he marked out their appointed times in history and the boundaries of their lands.

27 God did this so that they would seek him and perhaps reach out for him and find him, though he is not far from any one of us. 28 'For in him we live and move and have our being.' As some of your own poets have said, 'We are his offspring.'

29 Therefore since we are God's offspring, we should not think that the divine being is like gold or silver or stone—an image made by human design and skill. 30 In the past God overlooked such ignorance, but now he commands all people everywhere to repent. 31 For he has set a day when he will judge the world with justice by the man he has appointed. He has given proof of this to everyone by raising him from the dead."

Narrator

32 When they heard about the resurrection of the dead, some of them sneered, but others said,

Athenian Philosophers

"We want to hear you again on this subject."

Narrator

33 At that, Paul left the Council. 34 Some of the people became followers of Paul and believed. Among them was Dionysius, a member of the Areopagus, also a woman named Damaris, and a number of others.

Comparing the Ministry Approaches of Jesus and Paul

Paul did not anchor his approach to reaching others in his personality, his preferences, his cultural bias, or the Greek emphasis on mere logic. His ministry replicated, albeit in a different style, Jesus' basic incarnational approach. Paul, like Jesus, went to where the people were, found common ground, spoke in words and images they could understand, and called people to a new way of thinking, living, and loving.

The chart below provides a comparison between Paul's four steps modeled in Athens (column 1) and Jesus' return to his hometown synagogue in Luke 4:16ff (column 2).

Paul's Approach in Athens	Jesus Preaching to the Hometown Crowd
Step 1 was to **go**, stay with, be an example, listen, empathize, and ask questions of those he wanted to reach.	Jesus **went** back to his hometown, where he knew the people well and had listened to and loved them for many years.
Step 2 was to **affirm** the good in what the people already do or believe.	In sharing from Isaiah 61, Jesus indirectly **affirms** they are right to look for the Messiah who will bring salvation.
Step 3 was to make the gospel clear and relevant by using **familiar** words and images.	The Isaiah 61 passage Jesus shared was **familiar** to them—one of their favorite writings.
Step 4 was to **challenge** them to believe in Jesus and to think and act differently.	Jesus **challenged** them to think differently about the nature of the Messiah's mission and who should be welcomed: unlikely Gentiles.

Live into the Story

God

God's desire to reach all people led Paul to clearly show the skeptical Athenians that Jesus was superior to their "gods." Fill in the three sections below together as a group:

▶ Pick an idol in today's culture:

_____

▶ List two legitimate needs people are mistakenly hoping this idol will meet:

_____

_____

▶ Address ignorance: How does Jesus meet each of those same needs in a way the idol cannot?

_____

_____

Our Story

Like Paul, we need an incarnational approach to reach the diverse people in our globalized world. Based on your experience, personality, and fears, which of Paul's four steps below come most easily to you? Which is most challenging? Mark or note these below, then please explain.

▶ To **go**, stay with, be an example, listen, empathize, and ask questions of those I want to reach

▶ To **affirm** the good in what the people already do or believe

▶ To **contextualize** God's truth, making it clear and relevant by using familiar words and images

▶ To **challenge** them to believe in Jesus and then to think and act differently

1. The step that comes *easiest* to me:

_____

_____

2. The step that comes *hardest* to me:

_____

_____

Reaching Others

Refer to the answers of the **What Is Your Experience** question. Choose one segment of your local community that seems resistant or uninterested in Jesus and his message. Then, imagine you are part of a ministry team focused on reaching them. How might Paul's four-step example guide your initial efforts? Be as specific and practical as possible.

_____

_____

_____

_____

_____

_____

Close Together in Prayer

Looking Ahead

Paul's missionary journeys extended to the end of his life, and the church continued to grow after his passing. As the church matured, spiritual challenges and internal struggles surfaced—each one met by God's faithful guidance. Around 30 years later, while exiled on the island of Patmos, John received the Revelation from God. After addressing seven specific churches in Asia Minor, Scripture records no further direct messages from God to his people. We now live in this in-between time, guided by the Holy Spirit speaking through God's written Word and the life of Jesus. As we study the coming passages, we wait in hope for the story's promised conclusion.

Prayer Ideas

▸ Read Psalm 23. Notice that David, like Paul in his sermon, used language that people in his time would have been familiar with: sheep and shepherds.

▸ Reflect for a moment and then thank God for the people who came to you and, by their witness, made Jesus relatable and attractive.

▸ Pray that God would send more workers to the people groups of your community that are more resistant to Jesus and his message.

Action Ideas

▸ Write a short letter to God expressing your heart's burden, your motivation, and some specific steps you might take to engage a real or imagined group that is resistant to Jesus and his message. Share your letter with someone.

▸ Meet up with a friend and brainstorm some modern cultural messages or images that people your age can relate to and could be used in your communication of the gospel.

Discipleship Practice

▸ **Contextualizing the Gospel** | Communicating the timeless truths of Scripture in culturally relevant ways. It involves studying the target culture, identifying connection points between the gospel and local beliefs, and adapting the message and the approach accordingly. *Why?* It helps remove unnecessary barriers to the gospel message and cultivates a more fruitful ministry.

MYSIA
ADRAMYTTIUM
PERGAMOS
THYATIRA
SARDIS
SMYRA
LYDIA
EPHESUS
CARIA
MILETUS
PATMOS
RHODES

THE FIFTH ANGEL POURED OUT HIS BOWL
ON THE THRONE OF THE BEAST AND ITS
KINGDOM WAS PLUNGED INTO DARKNESS.

REVELATION 16:10

God's Love Brings Justice at Last

REVELATION 16:1-21

PURPOSE

1. To explore how God's final judgment balances justice and mercy to fulfill his redemptive purposes for creation.

2. To persevere in love, faith, and hope through the trials and persecution of this age.

MEMORY VERSE

Yes, O Lord God, the Almighty, your judgments are true and just! (Revelation 16:7)

KINGDOM THEME

God's Judgment of Evil

DISCIPLESHIP PRACTICE

Repentance

PRAYER

Lord, help me see the surprising reality of your judgment. Hear my prayer for those who need to know that even your final judgment is a part of holy love for the world.

Introduction

Though the writing of the Bible ended long ago, God's story continues to unfold. Sometimes, the church inspires, and sometimes it falls short. Yet, through it all, Jesus has never stopped shepherding his people.

Every Christ follower is invited to join the global mission of expanding the church and spreading the gospel. Our calling is to make disciples who, in turn, make more disciples, bringing the light of Christ to the world.

The ending of any story is critical, especially one that has kept you utterly captivated. *But what about the biblical story? What about God's story here in our world? How does it end? Can we know?*

The Book of Revelation gives us a glimpse of that finale. Part one of the conclusion reveals God's dramatic act of justice and his judgment of evil.

To fully grasp Revelation's message, we must see it in the context of the entire biblical narrative, where judgment plays a key role in confronting evil and restoring justice.

God's judgment isn't new in the Bible. In Genesis, Adam and Eve are mercifully expelled from Eden for their disobedience. Soon after, the flood wipes away a corrupt world, sparing only Noah and his family. Egypt suffered ten plagues from God's hand for enslaving the Hebrews. The Israelites who worshiped the golden calf perished at Mount Sinai. Later, God handed Israel over to the Assyrians and Babylonians for their repeated rebellion.

The prophets warned of God's judgment and discipline if rebellious Israel did not repent. Even Jesus warned of judgment for those who reject his message, and Paul openly speaks of God's judgment.

How does the Bible describe God's judgment, and what distinguishes the final judgment?

In Revelation 16, we witness God's final outpouring of judgment on the earth. Revelation unfolds as the last chapter of a 66-book story, where the final experience of evil's judgment completes what came before. While the communication style may differ, the foundation remains the same: God's judgment flows from his holiness and mercy.

Revelation's vision of evil's final judgment brought hope for the early church as they faced persecution, obstacles, and the temptation of wealth. Throughout history, Christians have found strength in this message while enduring evil rulers and hardships.

Not everyone, however, sees God's judgment in a positive light. Some view it as a sign of Jesus' anger or unloving nature. Others believe that after the Old Testament, Jesus replaced God's judgment with only unconditional love, forgiveness, and inclusion.

By looking closely at Revelation 16, we can explore how God's justice, loving discipline, and final judgment are interconnected with Christ's love and redemption. Understanding this can help us see God's true character in both his judgment and grace.

Background Help for Revelation

Revelation belongs to the genre of apocalyptic literature, which uses vivid symbols, striking imagery, and dramatic scenes to reveal spiritual realities and God's ultimate purposes. Rather than unfolding in a strict chronological sequence, apocalyptic writing presents a sweeping, symbolic vision of what is truly at stake in history.

This genre is sharply dualistic, contrasting light and darkness, good and evil, with little room for ambiguity. The faithful are often portrayed as a vulnerable minority standing against overwhelming opposition. Written in a context of persecution, Revelation was meant to strengthen early Christians by placing their suffering within a larger cosmic conflict and assuring them that, though victory was not yet visible, God's justice and triumph were certain.

What Is Your Experience?

Most cultures affirm the value of law and order. When law and order are done well, people generally respect the rulings of fair courts.

However, the word "judgment" can also trigger negative impressions and emotions. Our 21st-century value of tolerance leads many to ask, *"What gives us the right to judge another person?"* This mindset can lead some to view God's judgment as harsh or unloving.

▸ What comes to your mind when you hear "judging" or "judgment"?

_____

_____

Explore the Story

Consider the Viewpoints | Revelation 16:1-21

Your group leader will assign you a character from the four below. Notice what your character does and says, and then imagine their thoughts and feelings. Share some of your discussion highlights, any lingering questions, and how you can possibly relate to this character.

EVIL

Even before creation, Satan made himself God's enemy. His reign on earth is allowed for a season of time but will come to an end on the final judgment day. Satan's earthly kingdom will collapse, and his grip will be shaken loose, by the outpouring of God's judgments.

PEOPLE WHO REJECT GOD'S RULE

There have always been people who stand against God and resist his Kingdom rule. At the end, when Jesus reveals himself as King, there will continue to be those who rebel against his authority, refuse to repent, and curse God – even to his face. Those who follow the "Beast" and lead masses of people toward evil and destruction bear more of sin's responsibility and the consequences of judgment.

GOD'S PEOPLE PERSEVERE IN TRIALS

In every generation that has experienced suffering or persecution, a remnant of God's people remains steadfast. God's faithful people long for Christ's return, hoping his judgment will change their persecutors' hearts.

GOD THE FATHER AND GOD THE SON

God's holiness, justice, and judgments have always been inseparable from his love. As the Risen Lamb and the Lion of Judah, Jesus has been given all authority on earth and in heaven (Matthew 28:18). He alone has been entrusted by the Father to carry out divine judgment on the world.

Narrator

16:1 Then I heard a loud voice from the temple saying to the seven angels,

Voice From the Temple

"Go, pour out the seven bowls of God's wrath on the earth."

(Scripture continues on the next page)

Narrator

[2] *The first angel went and poured out his bowl on the land, and ugly, festering sores broke out on the people who had the mark of the beast and worshiped its image.*

[3] *The second angel poured out his bowl on the sea, and it turned into blood like that of a dead person, and every living thing in the sea died.*

[4] *The third angel poured out his bowl on the rivers and springs of water, and they became blood.* [5] *Then I heard the angel in charge of the waters say:*

Angel of the Waters

"You are just in these judgments, O Holy One, you who are and who were; [6] *for they have shed the blood of your holy people and your prophets, and you have given them blood to drink as they deserve."*

Voice from the Altar

[7] *"Yes, Lord God Almighty, true and just are your judgments."*

Narrator

[8] *And the fourth angel poured out his bowl on the sun, and the sun was allowed to scorch people with fire.* [9] *They were seared by the intense heat and they cursed the name of God, who had control over these plagues, but they refused to repent and glorify him.*

[10] *The fifth angel poured out his bowl on the throne of the beast, and its kingdom was plunged into darkness. People gnawed their tongues in agony* [11] *and cursed the God of heaven because of their pains and their sores, but they refused to repent of what they had done.*

[12] *The sixth angel poured out his bowl on the great river Euphrates, and its water was dried up to prepare the way for the kings from the East.*

[13] *Then I saw three impure spirits that looked like frogs; they came out of the mouth of the dragon, out of the mouth of the beast and out of the mouth of the false prophet.* [14] *They are demonic spirits that perform signs, and they go out to the kings of the whole world, to gather them for the battle on the great day of God Almighty.*

Jesus

[15] *"Behold, I am coming like a thief. Blessed is the one who stays awake and keeps his clothes, so that he will not walk about naked and people will not see his shame."*

Narrator

[16] *Then they gathered the kings together to the place that in Hebrew is called Har-Magedon. [17] The seventh angel poured out his bowl into the air, and out of the temple came a loud voice from the throne.,*

Voice From the Temple

"It is done!"

Narrator

[18] *Then there came flashes of lightning, rumblings, peals of thunder and a severe earthquake. No earthquake like it has ever occurred since mankind has been on earth, so tremendous was the quake. [19] The great city split into three parts, and the cities of the nations collapsed. God remembered Babylon the Great and gave her the cup filled with the wine of the fury of his wrath. [20] Every island fled away and the mountains could not be found. [21] From the sky huge hailstones, each weighing about a hundred pounds, fell on people. And they cursed God on account of the plague of hail, because the plague was extremely severe.*

REVELATION 16:1-21

THE BIGGER STORY
Parallels Between Exodus and Revelation

Some of the judgments in Revelation 16 are similar in kind and intensity to the Exodus plagues God brought upon a stubborn Egypt (Exodus 7-12). Both accounts share these in common:

▶ Water turns to blood; hailstones and boils harm the people.

▶ The plagues invite repentance for evil leaders who brought injustice and hardship upon God's people. Yet, the Pharaoh and his advisors only harden their hearts against Moses and God.

▶ God's suffering people need hope that one day, oppressive leaders will be brought to justice.

▶ The message to Pharaoh and the Beast is clear: God is superior to their gods and armies.

 # Live into the Story

God

What are several truths about God's character that you see in Revelation 16?

_____

_____

_____

_____

How would you now respond if someone asked you the question, _"So if God is truly merciful and loving, why would he judge and bring suffering the world?"_

_____

_____

_____

_____

Our Story

How might you think or act differently if you kept God's future judgment of evil close to your heart?

_____

_____

_____

Reaching Others

Imagine having the opportunity to share the truths of God's judgment as revealed in Revelation 16 with a small group of young believers. How might you communicate the meaning of this passage and its significance? What symbols, ideas, or stories could you use to help convey its message clearly and meaningfully?

_____

_____

_____

Imagine how they might respond to you sharing a message like this.

_____

_____

Looking Ahead

God's righteous judgment of evil is not the end of God's story—it is the necessary clearing of the stage for something far greater. As the forces of darkness are dismantled and justice is fully served, the way is prepared for the breathtaking arrival of God's kingdom on earth. Heaven is not merely a distant realm, but a reality poised to break in and renew the earth itself. In this final movement, everything broken will be restored, every sorrow healed, and all creation made new. And this glorious unveiling, promised by the One who is faithful and true, is not far off. It is coming...soon.

Theory to Practice: *Response for Disciples*

Prayer Ideas

▸ Read Psalm 97. Imagine yourself as a member of a 1st century house church living under Roman persecution. You have just had a reading of Revelation 16 and are responding by singing together Psalm 97, a song sung by God's people for centuries. How does this Psalm speak to you?

▸ Ask the Lord how knowing his final judgment of evil might lead us to pray for ourselves...for the lost...for persecuted Christians around the world...and for their persecutors. Take a few minutes to pray.

Action Ideas

▸ In the coming week, choose one or two fellow believers and share your key takeaways from Revelation 16. Talk together about what you believe to be true and significant about God's judgment—especially his final judgment of evil. Ask for their perspective and what has shaped it. Afterward, reflect on your conversation.

▸ Imagine an institution, a group, or an organization that consistently points people you know away from God's will. What would repentance look like for them? Write this all out in four to five sentences.

Discipleship Practice

▸ **Repentance** | Genuine awareness and sorrow for our sins lead us to turn away from harmful thinking and acting *and* toward Christ's better way. *Why?* Sinful patterns and a holy God require his power but also our decision if we are to experience forgiveness, freedom, humility, and integrity.

MYSIA
ADRAMYTTIUM
TROAS
PERGAMOS
THYATIRA
SARDIS
PHILAD
SMYRA
LYDIA
LA
EPHES
COLOS
CARIA
MILETUS
PATMOS
CNIDUS
RHODES

I HEARD A LOUD VOICE FROM THE THRONE SAYING, "GOD'S DWELLING PLACE IS NOW AMONG THE PEOPLE. HE IS MAKING EVERYTHING NEW!"

REVELATION 21:3, 5

A New Heaven and a New Earth

REVELATION 21-22:5

PURPOSE

1. To challenge our misconceptions and deepen our biblical understanding of heaven.

2. To inspire our hearts to hope in God's future new heaven and new earth—a hope that helps us endure life's hardest moments.

MEMORY VERSE

I saw the Holy City, the New Jerusalem, coming down out of heaven from God, prepared as a bride beautifully dressed for her husband. (Revelation 21:2)

KINGDOM THEME

Hope

DISCIPLESHIP PRACTICE

Waiting on God

PRAYER

Spirit of God, fill my heart's imagination with the truth of heaven. Make it clear why the hope of your future coming can change my life today...and tomorrow.

Introduction

In our previous lesson, we received good news: Jesus' final victory over sin, death, and evil's opposition to God is coming *soon*. Those who perpetuate evil will face final judgment, which is, at the same time, a merciful last chance to repent.

But what happens after that?

Like any great novel or movie, the Bible ends with a grand culmination of all that has unfolded. In the final chapters of Revelation, the Garden of Eden reappears, now full and expanded in the New Jerusalem on earth.

The final two chapters of Revelation, filled with rich symbolism and vivid imagery, address the frequently asked question: *What will life be like in heaven after we die?*

If you asked 100 people about heaven, you'd get a wide range of answers—some might describe it as a place of eternal peace and joy, while others might envision it as a realm of spiritual growth and learning. Some think it will be an amusement park of our own making. Most of these ideas are drawn from personal preferences or somebody's imagination.

Misunderstandings about heaven are rampant. Beyond misunderstanding heaven comes neglect.

Most people, even followers of Jesus, tend to avoid thinking deeply about life after death—unless they are suffering and need a strong hope for the future.

This need for hope was the situation of those who first heard the Book of Revelation. John's vision of God's coming kingdom motivated believers to endure persecution and suffering. Persevering with prayerful hope is what the Bible calls *waiting on God* (Isaiah 40:30-31).

Throughout history, people have waited on God, yearning for a better future; today is no different. We place our hope in what we believe will bring us closer to that brighter reality. Yet, for many, hope in our country's future, our leaders, institutions, economy, and even the church is fading fast.

In a world filled with growing hostility and uncertainty, John's powerful vision of heaven speaks to us with fresh urgency.

What Is Your Experience?

Share or write in at least one idea you have thought or heard about heaven for each question below.

1. Who and what will be present in heaven?

   _____

   _____

2. What will our relationships be like with each other? With the created world?

   _____

   _____

3. What will God be like, and what will our relationship be like with him?

   _____

   _____

4. What will people do?

   _____

   _____

Explore the Story

Consider the Viewpoints | Revelation 21-22:5

Your group leader will assign you a character from the four below. Notice what your character does and says, and then imagine their thoughts and feelings. Share some of your discussion highlights, any lingering questions, and how you can possibly relate to this character.

EVIL

Just before the arrival of the great New Jerusalem, the former great city of Babylon was destroyed. Her ruler, the devil, is dethroned. The coming to earth of the holy new heaven involves the elimination of all evil from her midst.

THE NATIONS AND THEIR LEADERS

City gates traditionally remained closed to protect its inhabitants from outside danger day and night. Gates of the New Jerusalem are always open (Revelation 21:25), perhaps because there is neither danger nor night. People from all nations stream to the city and are welcomed forever as part of God's people. Read Isaiah 2:2-3, for an Old Testament prophesy that will be fulfilled here.

PEOPLE OF GOD

Those who trust and obey God until the end will find their hope coming true. Their names will be written in the Book of Life. They will fully participate in the pleasures and shalom of the new heaven and earth.

GOD

The God who created this world and has long shown patience and love will have the final word. One day, when his kingdom comes fully to earth, he will make his dream—and ours—come true.

Narrator

21:1 Then I saw a new heaven and a new earth, for the first heaven and the first earth had passed away, and there was no longer any sea. 2 I saw the Holy City, the new Jerusalem, coming down out of heaven from God, prepared as a bride beautifully dressed for her husband. 3 And I heard a loud voice from the throne saying,

Loud Voice From the Throne

"Look! God's dwelling place is now among the people, and he will dwell with them. They will be his people, and God himself will be with them and be their God. 4 'He will wipe every tear from their eyes. There will be no more death or mourning or crying or pain, for the old order of things has passed away."

(Scripture continues on the next page.)

God Seated on the Throne

⁵ *"I am making everything new! Write this down, for these words are trustworthy and true. ⁶ It is done. I am the Alpha and the Omega, the Beginning and the End. To the thirsty I will give water without cost from the spring of the water of life. ⁷ Those who are victorious will inherit all this, and I will be their God and they will be my children. ⁸ But the cowardly, the unbelieving, the vile, the murderers, the sexually immoral, those who practice magic arts, the idolaters and all liars—they will be consigned to the fiery lake of burning sulfur. This is the second death."*

Narrator

⁹ *One of the seven angels who had the seven bowls full of the seven last plagues came and said to me,*

Angel

"Come, I will show you the bride, the wife of the Lamb."

Narrator

¹⁰ *And he carried me away in the Spirit to a mountain great and high, and showed me the Holy City, Jerusalem, coming down out of heaven from God. ¹¹ It shone with the glory of God, and its brilliance was like that of a very precious jewel, like a jasper, clear as crystal. ¹² It had a great, high wall with twelve gates, and with twelve angels at the gates. On the gates were written the names of the twelve tribes of Israel. ¹⁴ The wall of the city had twelve foundations, and on them were the names of the twelve apostles of the Lamb... ²² I did not see a temple in the city, because the Lord God Almighty and the Lamb are its temple. ²³ The city does not need the sun or the moon to shine on it, for the glory of God gives it light, and the Lamb is its lamp. ²⁴ The nations will walk by its light, and the kings of the earth will bring their splendor into it. ²⁵ On no day will its gates ever be shut, for there will be no night there. ²⁶ The glory and honor of the nations will be brought into it. ²⁷ Nothing impure will ever enter it, nor will anyone who does what is shameful or deceitful, but only those whose names are written in the Lamb's Book of Life.*

Note: vv. 13 and 15-21 have been omitted for study purposes.

22:1 Then the angel showed me the river of the water of life, as clear as crystal, flowing from the throne of God and of the Lamb 2 down the middle of the great street of the city. On each side of the river stood the tree of life, bearing twelve crops of fruit, yielding its fruit every month. And the leaves of the tree are for the healing of the nations. 3 No longer will there be any curse. The throne of God and of the Lamb will be in the city, and his servants will serve him. 4 They will see his face, and his name will be on their foreheads. 5 There will be no more night. They will not need the light of a lamp or the light of the sun, for the Lord God will give them light. And they will reign for ever and ever.

REVELATION 21-22:5

THE BIGGER STORY
Old Testament Allusions

The Old and New Testaments are alluded to or directly cited ***hundreds of times*** in the book of Revelation. Revelation is the pulling together of the whole biblical story. Good examples are Revelation 21:1, 2, and 4, verses directly referencing Isaiah 65:17 and 19: *"For I am about to create new heavens and a new earth; the former things shall not be remembered or come to mind .... I will rejoice over Jerusalem and take delight in my people; the sound of weeping and of crying will be heard in it no more."*

Passages from Revelation should therefore be interpreted with the whole biblical story in mind. This keeps its readers from many unhelpful conclusions about the meaning of its images and symbols.

Live into the Story

God

Here is a summary list from Revelation 21 and 22 of the metaphors and symbolic descriptions of God and the new heaven and earth:

▶ God's people are one holy bride and married forever to God.

▶ Jesus is the Lamb of God, worshiped on the throne as reigning King.

▶ We are the children of God; we are his people, and he is our God.

▶ The New Jerusalem has thick walls that symbolize protection and strength, yet its gates never close, showing openness and welcome.

▶ At the center of the city are the Lord Almighty and Jesus, the Lamb of God, making the old temple obsolete. God Himself is now our temple!

▶ God's continual light and presence means the sun has also become obsolete.

▶ Eden's Garden bears superabundant fruit and brings healing to the nations.

▶ A river of living water flows in the middle of the city; there is no more thirst.

▶ Night, the fearful sea, all forms of evil, tears, death, and suffering no longer exist.

What do these descriptions and metaphors imply about God's character? (List at least five)

1. _____
2. _____
3. _____
4. _____
5. _____

Our Story

Remember your imagined description of heaven in **What Is Your Experience** at the beginning of this lesson. How are the descriptions and heaven metaphors in Revelation 21-22 similar to or better than what you imagined? Please explain.

a. Similar: _____

_____

b. Better: _____

_____

Reaching Others

Sharing about heaven can be tricky because of people's misconceptions about it. At the same time, the need for a solid hope has never been greater. We face countless challenges: the threat of serious viruses, nuclear conflict, climate change, pollution, racism, corrupt leaders, distrust in institutions, poverty, the breakdown of families and communities, and an epidemic of violence, loneliness, and depression—just to name a few.

Choose one image of heaven from the list in the earlier **God** question. How does this image offer hope, comfort, and reassurance in a world that often feels uncertain and divided?

_____

_____

_____

_____

Close Together in Prayer

Looking Ahead

Though Scripture's written story has ended, God's kingdom story continues—and we are part of it! It's ours to carry forward. We are invited to step into it—to live it out with purpose, hope, and expectancy. With hearts awakened and eyes fixed on what's to come, we wait—not with passivity, but with purpose—for the day when all things are made new and heaven fills the world with God's glory!

Theory to Practice: *Response for Disciples*

Prayer Ideas

▸ Praise God that heaven will one day come to earth and that Jesus will fully restore everything broken here.

▸ Confess the sin of putting your future hope in another source besides God.

▸ Ask God to plant his hope of a new heaven and earth more deeply in your heart.

Action Ideas

▸ Identify a personal practice that could deepen the promise of heaven within you (journaling, meditation, prayer, scripture reading, memorization, music, art or poetry, e.g.). Pick two times in the week ahead when you could do this practice. Write down your plan.

▸ Imagine yourself as a Jesus follower living under severe persecution during the first century. Read Psalm 130:5-8, and imagine yourself as a night watcher on top of the city wall, ordered to look for any sign of an approaching enemy. You are waiting on God for his final rescue and promised salvation.

Discipleship Practice

▸ **Waiting on God** | Actively trusting in God's provision, timing, and sovereignty while we bring our need(s) to him, patiently anticipating his intervention. We wait in times of prayer and as a life posture. *Why?* It develops patience and submission, diminishes our impulsiveness, and aligns believers with God's perfect timing and better outcomes.

MYSIA

TROAS • ADRAMYTTIUM

★ PERGAMOS

★ THYATIRA

★ SARDIS

SMYRA ★ PHILAD
★ LYDIA

EPHESUS ★ ★ LA

CARIA CPLO

MILETUS •

PATMOS •

CNIDUS

RHODES

The Ups & Downs of God's Kingdom Story

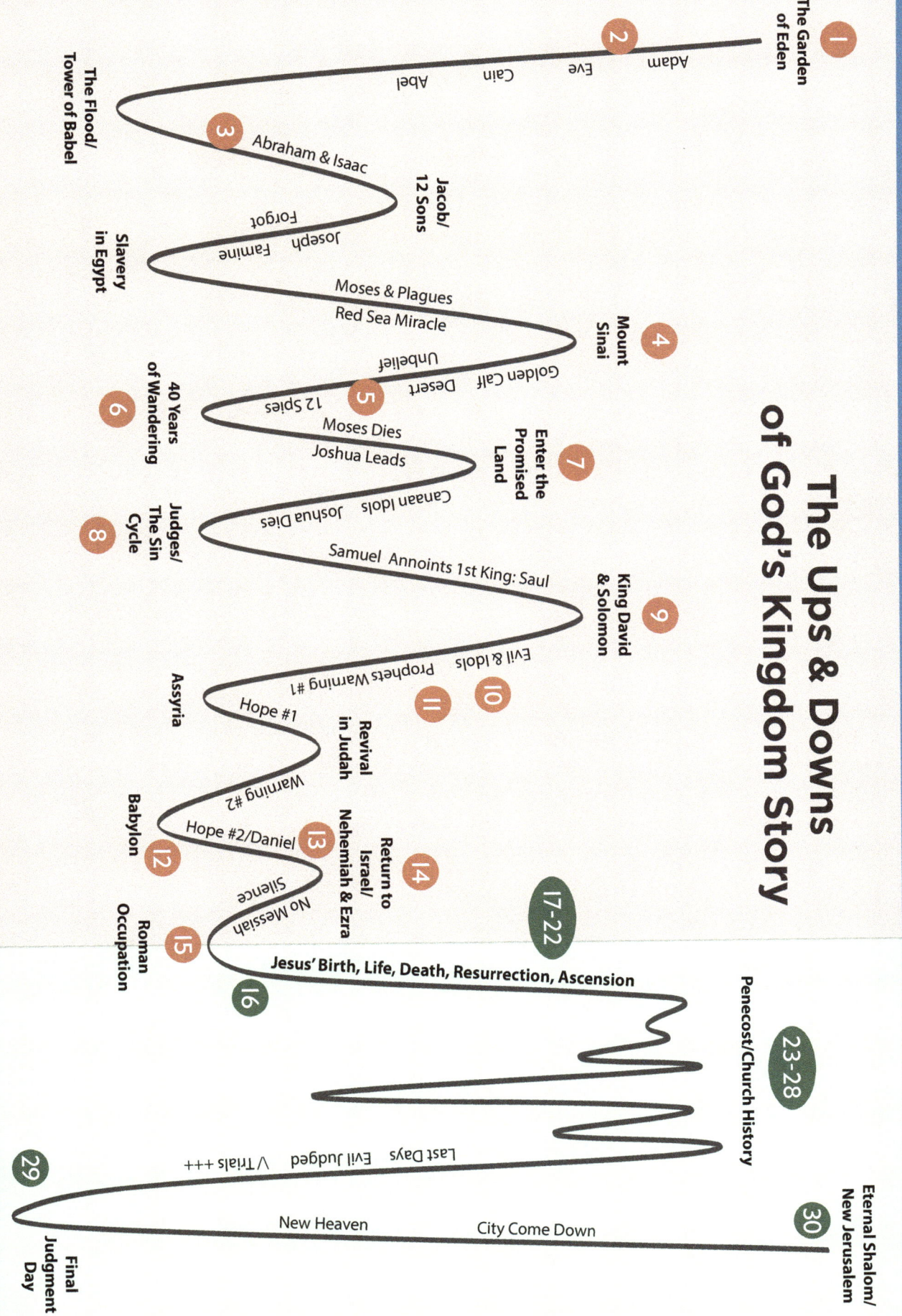

OLD TESTAMENT

NEW TESTAMENT

1 The Garden of Eden

2 Adam Eve Cain Abel

The Flood/ Tower of Babel

3 Abraham & Isaac

Jacob/ 12 Sons

Joseph Famine Forgot

Slavery in Egypt

Moses & Plagues
Red Sea Miracle

4 Mount Sinai

Golden Calf Desert Unbelief

5 12 Spies

6 40 Years of Wandering

Moses Dies
Joshua Leads

7 Enter the Promised Land

Canaan Idols Joshua Dies

8 Judges/ The Sin Cycle

Samuel Annoints 1st King: Saul

9 King David & Solomon

Evil & Idols

10 Prophets Warning #1

11 Revival in Judah

Assyria Hope #1

Warning #2

12 Babylon

13 Hope #2/Daniel

Silence No Messiah

14 Return to Israel/ Nehemiah & Ezra

15 Roman Occupation

16 Jesus' Birth, Life, Death, Resurrection, Ascension

17-22

23-28 Penecost/Church History

Last Days Evil Judged √ Trials +++

29 Final Judgment Day

New Heaven City Come Down

30 Eternal Shalom/ New Jerusalem

Acknowledgments

Every book requires a host of helpers, but a workbook facilitating a participatory experience of discipleship takes my indebtedness to a higher level.

The Kingdom Story Experience *is just that, an experience that has involved groups since 1994, people of many ages and several nationalities. Trial and error, drafts and redrafts, happened continuously over the last three decades; every group of these yearly experiences has in its own way helped me shape what you will find in this material. There have been no lack of honest critics and cheerleaders along the way. It has taken a village.*

Another collage of friends and strategic partners have taken time to edit, rewrite, type set, and give me important feedback over the last 4 decades: Paul Allen, Jen Dean, Levi Edgecombe, Matt Allen, Arthur Koh, Arlyn Lawerence, Cody Lail, Andrew Hilzendeger, Denee Curl, Jennifer Tabert, and Connie Willems, and I am sure I have forgotten a few.

Two people stand out: many long, honest conversations and thoughtful feedback with co-teacher Branden Hubbell have brought the KSE to a sharper focus it so desperately needed. Kami Wright took on the project of a modern re-design and spent hours working on artwork, formatting, and taking in my incessant "last-minute" edits—and all with good cheer and encouragement! Branden and Kami's contributions have proved valuable beyond measure.

I am most indebted to my living King Jesus Christ. This publication is to me a living reminder of God's faithfulness to weave together some of the messy, miraculous, and mundane stories of my ministry years. Teaching The Kingdom Story Way *(the first iteration of what you hold now) has been, I must admit, in no small part selfish; it is hard to imagine my life apart from being tethered, again and again and again, to Christ's Spirit through the people and experiences of The Kingdom Story.*

— John